The Deaf to Deaf killings

Peter W. Jackson

First published in Great Britain 2010

Copyright © Peter Jackson 2010

Published by
Deafprint Winsford
Winsford
Cheshire
CW7 3UD
England

The right of the Peter Webster Jackson to be identified as the author of this work has been asserted by him in accordance with the Copyright, Designs and Patents Act, 1988.

All rights reserved
No part of this publication may be reproduced by any means, or stored in or introduced into a retrieval system, or transmitted in any form or by any means (electronic, mechanical, photocopying, recording or otherwise) without the prior written permission of the copyright owner and the above publisher of this book.

British Library Cataloguing Data

ISBN 978-0-9562288-1-9

Printed in England by JEM Digital Print Services, Sittingbourne, Kent ME10 2NH

To

Maureen

Other Crime Books by Peter Jackson

Deaf Crime Casebook
Deaf to Evidence
Deaf Murder Casebook
Deaf Target
Death Around the Green
Deaf Killers
Deaf Injustices
Deaf Executions

History Books

Britain's Deaf Heritage
A Pictorial History of Deaf Britain
A History of the Deaf Community in Northwich and Winsford 1880 – 2002
(with Maureen Jackson)
Deaf Lives (Ed. with Raymond Lee)
Manchester Memoirs (Ed.)
Preston Pride (with Maureen Jackson)
The Gawdy Manuscripts

Contents

Chapter		Page
	Acknowledgements	vii
	Introduction	1
1.	Raped & Murdered in Her Bed France	3
2.	A Scandal in a Small Village Germany	7
3.	Murder and Arson Australia	13
4.	The Man Who Thought He Had Got Away With Murder Denmark	19
5.	The 27-Year Cold Case Illinois, USA	27
6.	Jealousy Led to a Bloody Murder! Australia	33
7.	The Burnt Body France	37
8.	The Body on the Back Porch Decking North Carolina, USA	43
9	A Question of Legality of a Confession in Sign Language Michigan, USA	49

10	Cut up and Scattered on a Landfill Site Poland	61
11	A Shotgun Settles an Argument Pennsylvania, USA	69
12	The Sioux Falls Chainsaw Murder South Dakota	77
13	Murder in a Deaf Town Illinois, USA	97
14	The Fatal Shooting that Ended a 24-year Relationship Michigan, USA	105
15	The Abuse Germany	111
16	The Seductress Hong Kong	119
17	Gangs of Thieves, Kidnappings and Murders China	124
18	A Rapist Poisoned, Cut to Pieces and Burnt Peru	145

Acknowledgements

There have been many people who have contributed to this book in a variety of ways, starting with the help I have received from my interpreter/communicators, Samantha Anderson and Pauline Tolfree. I am grateful for their patience in putting up with me whilst on research tours.

Some of these stories could not have been written without the contributions from the following people, some of whom did research on my behalf:
- Bernard Le Maire
- Breda Carty
- Ed Hoyt
- Gordon Hay
- Lothar Scharf
- Simon Hesselberg
- Wendy Woodwardson

I am grateful to Mark Lewis for giving me the idea and explaining how to research deaf-related murder cases from non-English speaking countries on the Internet; Google and the Google translation facility are indeed wonderful tools. This is how the stories from China, Peru, France and modern-day Germany became available.

I am indebted to Natasha Charles for some of the translations of German paperwork; and to Tereze Weiss for the translation of the magazine story from Denmark.

Thanks are also due to many individuals of various libraries, courthouses and schools for their time and patience in dealing with my enquiries and assisting in my research, especially:

- British Newspaper Library (Colindale, London);
- Hinsdale South High School (Illinois);
- Illinois State School for the Deaf (Jacksonville);
- Indian Prairie Public Library (Darien, Illinois);
- Jacksonville (Illinois) Public Library;
- Koszalińska Biblioteka Publiczna (Poland);
- Macomb County Circuit Court (Michigan);
- Morgan County Courthouse (Jacksonville, Illinois);
- Mount Clemens Public Library (Michigan);
- Palm Bay Public Library (Florida);
- Sioux Falls Public Library (South Dakota);
- Westland Police Department (Michigan);
- William P. Faust Public Library of Westland (Michigan)

It is indeed humbling to recall just how many people were so willing to put themselves out to assist me in my research.

As ever, I am grateful for the support received from my wife, Maureen, during the research and writing phases, especially during the three weeks we spent in the USA during September and October 2009, when we travelled thousands of miles gathering the case details and related photography for seven American stories.

To Jo Rourke, thanks for proof-reading the book and correcting some of the English. Any mistakes that remain are mine alone.

To all my readers, my great thanks. Without your enthusiasm for Deaf crime, there would be no motivation for me to write these stories.

Peter W. Jackson
Winsford, Cheshire
March 2010

Introduction

A newspaper reporter seeking to sensationalise her article linked to the trial of Daphne Wright (*see page 77*) blithely without checking her facts properly wrote that:

> ... *the murder of a deaf person by another deaf person is quite rare...*

As the stories told in this book show, this is balderdash.

Every story in this book involves a killing (or killings) of a Deaf person by another Deaf person.

It is a fact that a Deaf person is much more likely to be murdered by another Deaf person than by someone who is not Deaf.

I have many more stories of murders of Deaf people by Deaf people than which appear in this book, or that have appeared in my other books. Several factors prevent me from writing about all of them:

1. Some cases are very difficult to research due to distance, time, money and language barriers;
2. Many Deaf murderers or killers have been released from prison and are still walking around in various Deaf communities, some married, and some with Deaf family members, and it would be unfair to identify these people who have served their time for their crime.

3. In Europe, in particular, many murder cases that come to court and/or are reported in the media do not have the identities of the victims or the murderers shown in the official reports. This is particularly true of Dutch and German cases.

Nonetheless, the stories in this book, which come from all over the world, can be illustrative of the Deaf-to-Deaf murders that can happen.

Chapter 1:

Raped and Murdered in her bed!
Brittany, France 1900

Marie-Jeanne Appérè had a long and difficult life in the village of Prat-Allan, near Guincamp in Brittany. Apart from the time she was sent away to a school for the Deaf near Rennes where she spent three years, she had never been away from her village and had spent her working life as a domestic or as a washerwoman in various houses around Prat-Allan, making out a precarious living. As a poor deaf-mute, she habitually dressed in black rags and presented a pathetic and unattractive figure to other residents of Prat-Allan. Consequently, she never married.

Now 73 years old, she was no longer able to work, and lived in a poorhouse in the village, spending her days doing a bit of sewing to help make ends meet. Few people in the village were able to use any form of sign language with her, but in the late summer of 1900, a farm labourer named Goulven Jacquelin, aged 42 years, began to work on a local farm during the harvest. He was also, by definition, a deaf-mute and upon being told about the old deaf woman, he was able to provide Marie-Jeanne with some company and sign language conversation.

One night in September, Marie-Jeanne was asleep in her bed in her room when she was woken up by an intruder climbing into her bed. It was Goulven Jacquelin who had climbed in through an open window and was now trying to rape her. During the struggle, Goulven Jacquelin feared that the woman would denounce him after the rape, and in a frenzy, stabbed her five times on various parts of her body. He also tried to strange her with a rope that he had brought with him.

The commotion was heard by people in neighbouring rooms. At least one looked into Marie-Jeanne's room and saw Jacquelin on top of the old woman, but most neighbours were afraid to investigate until early in the morning when some of them were brave enough to venture into Marie-Jeanne Appérè's room. There, they found her stretched out on the floor in the form of a crucifix in a large pool of blood. She was still alive, and when a doctor was called out, he had her admitted to the nearest hospital as a matter of urgency, but a few days later, she died.

As a friend of Marie-Jeanne, and also the person seen to be on top of the old woman by the neighbour who looked into the room, Goulven Jacquelin was naturally wanted for questioning by the gendarmerie, who were called in to investigate the crime.

Goulven Jacquelin, however, was no longer to be found at the farm where he worked. His room showed signs of a hurried departure. He had not got very far from Prat-Allan when he was spotted and stopped on the road by some gendarmes. His clothes were blood-stained, and by gestures and signs, he soon made a full admission of the crime when taken back to Prat-Allan.

Goulven Jacquelin was transported to Brest, the main city in Brittany, for trial but his deafness caused some problems as the magistrate found that there was no-one in the area able to interpret at the trial.

Brest around 1900

Instead, a decision was made by the Magistrates in Brest that there was sufficient proof he was the murderer of Marie-Jeanne Appérè, but they were in a quandary. What were they to do with him when he could not have a fair trial?

Instead, the court in Brest ordered him to be placed in a lunatic asylum for life.

The Port of Brest was home to some of France's most notorious prisons, but most of these were closed when the infamous Devil's Island and the prison colony of French Guinea were established in the late 19th century, but because Goulven Jacquelin had not really been found guilty, he was fortunate that he was not sent there.

The famous French penal colony on Devils Island
off the coast of South America.

Chapter 2:

A Scandal in a small village
Germany 1915

Witze in the Brandenburg region of Germany is a very small hamlet about 12 kilometres north of Rathenow, a main town in an area of many small farming communities. Although a modern housing development has now sprung up on the outskirts of the village, the area in the centre of the village, particularly around the old timber-framed church is much as what it was in 1862 when Hermann Ide was born on a cold wintry morning on 4 February to Guenther and Hildegard Ide, who owned a smallholding near the church in Witze.

When he was four years old, little Hermann developed a fever which led to him being diagnosed afterwards as deaf and dumb, and in an effort to give him an education, his parents sent him to the K. Deaf and Dumb Institute in Berlin, where he learnt to communicate in sign language. This was despite the time being the era where education through Oralism (or the 'German Method' as it was known in the rest of Europe and America) was beginning to be dominant, leading to the banning of the use of Sign Language as a means of communication and education in schools.

Hermann left school at the age of 14 or 15, and was apprenticed to an ophthalmic factory in Rathenow where he helped to make spectacles and spectacle frames for those who had eyesight problems. However, he did not enjoy working in a factory, and rejoined the family farm which was now being run by his elder brother.

The Ide family farm in Witze

In due course, Hermann Ide grew up to become a respected member of the deaf community in the north Brandenburg region centred on Rathenow, which had a place of worship for local deaf people. There was another place of worship and social organisation in Kyritz, a town about 40 kilometres north of Rathenow, run by a Father Petschow who prevailed upon Hermann Ide to become the chairman of the local deaf organisation, a position he held for many years.

Although well-known and well-respected, Hermann Ide found one matter beyond him – he could never find a woman to share his life with and reached the age of 50 still unmarried. In his fiftieth year, however, he got to know Minna Fehlow, a member of the deaf congregation at the church in Rathenow.

Born on 17 April 1892 and therefore at least 30 years younger than Hermann Ide, the girl was unemployed and still living at home with her parents, and was anxious to escape them in order to achieve some independence. Using his position as the respected chairman of the local deaf organisation, Hermann arranged for Minna to enter into service with a farmer in Witze named Zander, for whom she subsequently did the washing, cleaning and doing general jobs about the Zander farm.

It was 1915 and the first world war was raging in Flanders, but all this was remote to Hermann Ide because having another Deaf person in the small community of Witze did wonders for him; for the first time in his home life, he now had someone he could communicate with in sign language on a daily basis, usually after they both had finished their daily tasks on their respective farms. Minna came to be regarded by the villagers as Hermann's girlfriend, and in natural consequence, they became lovers.

Perhaps inevitably, Minna became pregnant and naturally asked Hermann what he proposed to do about her situation. However, Hermann became suspicious that Minna had been distributing her favours amongst other, much younger, men in the village and the baby might not be his. Minna had transferred employment to another farmer named Heitepriem, who was more of her age and might have been availing himself of her services in more ways than one. Hermann became reluctant to incur the cost of bringing up the baby, or indeed to marry Minna Fehlow and bring up the baby as his.

He agonised for weeks about his dilemma, whilst Minna Fehlow's condition became more and more obvious and the villagers were looking at him to do the honourable thing. On 1st August 1915, Minna Fehlow disappeared; she did not turn up to do the daily tasks required of her by the farmer Heitepriem. To add to the mystery, Hermann Ide was nowhere to be found, but when he turned up, he said he had been to the town of Vietznitz on deaf organisation business and expressed concern about the disappearance of Minna Fehlow.

After a long search, the corpse of Minna Fehlow was found in boggy marshland mid-way between Witze and Rathenow; her head had been smashed in and she had been nearly decapitated.

After the discovery of the body, Hermann Ide ran from the village, pursued by a group of villagers convinced that he was responsible for the murder of the girl-servant. In trying to escape his pursuers, Hermann tried to drown himself in the marshlands but was pulled from the water and taken to the police court at Rathenow where he confessed to being the culprit of Fehlow's death, saying that he had met with her in the Heitepriem barn and clubbed her to death following another argument about her condition.

The Heitepriem barn in Witze where Hermann Ide clubbed Minna Fehlow to death

On Wednesday 8 December 1915, Hermann Ide stood before the High Court at Potsdam, the capital of the Brandenburg district of Germany, and was charged with the murder of Minna Fehlow. The court employed a teacher named Elisabeth Shenk from Charlottenburg as an interpreter, though apparently she did not manage the interpretation well, as the questioning of the accused in court became very long-winded and complicated.

In the end, the questioning, coupled with Hermann's admission of guilt, was enough for the court to find him guilty, though not of murder as the prosecution wanted, but of manslaughter, and he was sentenced to three years and four months in prison under mitigating circumstances, with the four months he had already spent in custody taken into account.

But for Hermann Ide, the loss of prestige and his standing as a respected member of the local Deaf community was more acutely felt than the fact of imprisonment.

Ein taubstummer Mörder.

Der Mordprozeß gegen den am 4. Februa 1864 zu Witzke geborenen taubstummen Land mann Hermann Ide wegen Tötung seiner eben falls taubstummen Geliebten, der am 17. April 1892 geborenen Dienstmagd Minna Fehlow worüber wir seinerzeit in No. 16 unseres Blatte vom 15. August vorigen Jahres ausführlich be richtet haben, kam am Mittwoch, den 8. De zember v. J. vor dem Potsdamer Schwurgerich zur Verhandlung. Vor Eingang in die Verhand lung wurde Fräulein Elisabeth Schenk au Charlottenburg als Dolmetscherin vereidigt, di

Part of a newspaper article detailing the story of the murder of Minna Fehlow.

Chapter 3:

Murder and Arson
Sydney, Australia 1961

No-one knows why, after many years of marriage, a person may snap and become violent and try to kill their spouse and possibly also other members of their family. It may be because of constant rows between husband and wife, or depression caused by misbehaving children, or problems at work. It could also be due to financial problems.

There does not have to be a prior history of domestic violence either, which makes it particularly shocking for friends, relatives or neighbours when a sudden outburst of violence results in murder or manslaughter, perhaps when the mind is disturbed and the killer cannot see any way out for himself or herself.

So, when neighbours called out the fire brigade to a burning house in the Sydney suburb of Ermington in the early hours of Wednesday morning 15 March 1961, they were shocked and appalled to discover what the firefighters found in the burning building. First, three young boys aged five, eight and thirteen were brought out and rushed to hospital suffering from smoke inhalation. A few minutes later, the father of the three boys was brought out but he was not allowed to go to hospital – instead he was treated at the scene by an ambulance crew who called out the police upon discovering suspicious wounds.

Lastly, a body was brought out covered in a blanket. After inspection by police officers called to the scene, it was taken away by ambulance to the Coroner's Office for a post-mortem.

The wounded man was found to need hospital treatment for wounds to his throat and wrists, and was taken there by another ambulance accompanied by a police officer. With the departure of the family from the burning house, it was subsequently doused and fire investigators accompanied by detectives then ventured into the house and brought out a mattock.

A mattock like the one used to kill Doreen Bushby

A mattock is a hand tool similar to a pickaxe. It is distinguished by the head, which makes it particularly suitable for digging or breaking up moderately hard ground. A mattock has a broad chisel-like blade perpendicular to the handle. This broad-bladed end is effectively an adze that could be used as a hoe as well. The reverse may have a pointed end, in which case the tool is called a pick mattock, or instead have an end with a three pronged axe like a fork. A combination axe and mattock used for fighting forest fires is a pulaski. It is sometimes called a "grub hoe".

Mattock heads range from 3to 7 lb in weight, and are normally mounted on a shaft three to four feet long. The shaft is often heavier than the head, sometimes possessing twice the mass and density of a baseball bat.

Mattocks are frequently used for path work in hill areas such as the Scottish Highlands, and are used extensively in archaeological excavation. It is a tool that is common in Australia.

Later the same day of Wednesday 15 March, Graham William Bushby, a 37-year-old cabinet-maker, appeared before the magistrates in the Parramatta Court of Petty Sessions charged with the murder of his wife, Doreen Marcella Bushby, also 37, and the attempted murder by fire of his three young boys. He was remanded in custody for five weeks to allow police enquiries to continue.

In a statement to the Press, a police spokesperson stated that Bushby had killed his wife by hitting her on the head with a mattock whilst she was sleeping on a sofa in the lounge. The accused had then slashed his throat and slit his wrists with a razor in a futile attempt to end his life.

Graham and Doreen Bushby had been childhood school sweethearts at the New South Wales Institution for the Deaf, Dumb and Blind at Newtown, Darlington, near Sydney and had been married for over 15 years at the time of the murder.

The NSW Institution for the Deaf, Darlington, Sydney.
This building is part of Sydney University, who have taken steps to preserve its remarkable architecture.
Both Graham and Doreen Bushby attended this school.

At the trial of Graham Bushby on Friday 11 August 1961 at the Central Criminal Court in Sydney before Mr. Justice Dovey, the court heard that although the victim's body was badly burnt by the attempted arson, the appalling injuries to the head that she suffered due to the force exerted through use of the mattock were quite apparent. The court also heard that Bushby was having psychiatric problems within his marriage and deeply regretted killing his wife, and trying to kill his sons.

He pled guilty to the manslaughter of Doreen Bushby, a plea agreed with the prosecutor's office. If he had not done this, and the case had gone to full trial, there was a risk that he would have received the death sentence, which was still in force in Australia at that time.

12 YEARS' GAOL FOR DEAF AND DUMB MAN

SYDNEY, Friday.—A deaf and dumb man, who killed his wife with a mattock and then set fire to their home while their three sons slept inside, was sentenced to 12 years' gaol in the Central Criminal Court today.

Passing sentence, Mr. Justice Dovey said he had to protect the man's children and others from possible repetition of similar violence.

He recommended that the father, Graham Bill Bushby, receive psychiatric treatment while in prison.

Bushby (37), a cabinet maker of the Sydney suburb of Ermington, pleaded guilty to the manslaughter of his wife, Doreen Marcel Bushby, who was also deaf and dumb, at their home on March 15.

Part of a newspaper report from the
West Australian newspaper dated 12 August 1961.
The case was also well-reported in Sydney newspapers.

Graham Bushby was sentenced to 12 years' imprisonment, which was to be served in the State's Long Bay Penitentiary at Malabar, New South Wales.

The Long Bay Penitentiary at Malabar, New South Wales.
(see also page 33)

In passing sentence, Mr. Justice Dovey said that he had a duty to protect the children of the marriage from possible repetition of similar violence and recommended that Bushby receive psychiatric treatment while in prison.

Chapter 4:

**The Man Who Thought He had Got Away with Murder
Denmark 1978**

Life under the then communist regime in Hungary in 1966 was grim, and the detested Soviet occupation forces made life uncomfortable and unbearable for most of the population. Deaf people in Hungary were no different from others in their suffering under that harsh regime. In one aspect, however, Deaf people were more fortunate than their hearing peers. International sport for Deaf people under the auspices of the *Comite Internationale des Sportes Sourds*, the world-wide organisation for Deaf Sport better known as the CISS, was flourishing and Deaf people in many Eastern European countries used the events organised by the CISS to experience travel and life outside the communist Eastern Bloc countries.

In 1966, Denmark also held the Secretariat of the CISS, and organised an event in the country to which a Hungarian Deaf team and their supporters were invited. Amongst the sports players and supporters was a 25-year-old Deaf man named Istvan Szabor. On arrival in Copenhagen, he immediately defected from the Hungarian Deaf team and sought political asylum.

The years immediately following the granting of the political asylum were lonely for Istvan Szabor. He knew no Danish, and although he used Hungarian Sign language, this was different from Danish Sign Language, so he had to learn both languages in order to communicate with others in Denmark, including Deaf people. In time, through special education classes, Szabor acquired some understanding of Danish and also learnt to communicate in Danish Sign Language. In addition, he got a job in an abattoir in Roskilde, a small town about 20 kilometres east of Copenhagen. He was progressing well and was regarded as a model citizen, so much so that he was granted Danish citizenship in 1974. There was, however, one void in his life – he was unable to find a partner to live with or to marry.

In the same year (1974), there was another international Deaf Sports event in Denmark and more Deaf people from Hungary defected, applying for political asylum. Among those applying for political asylum was a 22 year-old young woman named Gabriella Jálek.

Istvan Szabor was absolutely delighted to find a group of other Deaf people from his homeland, and in no time at all, he had ingratiated himself with Gabriella Jálek. Despite the disparity in ages, within months of meeting they were married. There were some advantages on both sides. In Istvan, Gabriella was getting a Hungarian-born Deaf man who had acquired Danish citizenship and who by now knew his way around Denmark and its language, and could therefore assist in helping her to blend into her new country. In Gabriella, Istvan was getting a pretty young woman from Hungary with whom he could converse in his native Hungarian Sign Language. It was probably more a marriage of convenience rather than of lasting love as the couple had only known each other a few short weeks.

Gabriella could not find a job in Roskilde, but was lucky enough to obtain work in the Royal Porcelain factory in Frederiksberg, a small town about 45 kilometres south-east of Roskilde. Today, the factory is known as Royal Copenhagen. It was a better paid job than Istvan's in the abattoir, so they moved to a small apartment in Smallegade, Frederiksberg.

The Royal Porcelain factory in Frederiksberg where Gabriella Szabor obtained employment

Istvan tried to keep his job in Roskilde by commuting to it from Frederiksberg, but the strain of early morning starts and late night returns commuting the 40-odd kilometres each way soon began to tell on him, and inevitably, after being constantly late or missing shifts, he was dismissed from his position in the abattoir.

The shame of having no job led to Istvan taking to the bottle in a big way, and Gabriella soon began to dread the daily wait at night for her drunken husband to return home from the numerous bars he frequented. The nightmare got worse when Istvan started to become violent and hit her as he pleased.

She would have left him, but she was really happy in the porcelain factory which became a place of refuge for her from the drunken Istvan. She was a much appreciated employee making friends with other colleagues, and became a member of the Ceramics Union.

Gabriella went to work on Monday 27 December 1976 as usual rather than stay at the apartment and be subjected to any violence from Istvan who had been drunk all through Christmas. However, she was feeling ill with a sore throat and the factory management decided to send her home at 11am.

The next thing that people could really be certain about was around 5 pm the same evening when an ambulance brought Gabriella to the emergency ward at Frederiksberg Hospital, which was quite near to her home in Smallegade. She was pronounced dead on arrival at 5:05pm, and as the doctors were unable to determine the cause of her death with any satisfaction, they referred the matter to the criminal police in Frederiksberg. When they attended the hospital, they found Istvan Szabor in the waiting area. When they found out he was Deaf, they called out for a sign language interpreter and kept him under observation until the interpreter's arrival.

Istvan Szabor

During questioning at the hospital, Istvan told the police that he had been out drinking all Boxing Day, not returning to his apartment until early in the morning. He was vaguely aware that Gabriella had left to go to work at 6am, but had slept through the day until he had woken up at some point in the afternoon and found his wife lying fully dressed on the floor next to the double bed. He had tried to shake her awake, but discovered that her body was cold.

After half-an-hour, Istvan left the apartment to find someone who could give him some help. It took him 20 minutes to find help. This was a man who agreed to follow him into the apartment and lift his wife onto the bed. As they did so, Istvan discovered a deep cut on the side of her throat and pointed this out to the man helping him, who then prudently called for an ambulance before making himself scarce.

The police had their doubts about Istvan's story, and requested that he accompany them to the police station where he was subjected to more questioning. Istvan quickly embroiled himself in some fanciful and ridiculous explanations, one of them being that when Gabriella had returned from work, she had found him in a faked seizure in the apartment and thought he was about to die, so she had chosen to commit suicide as she could simply not live without him.

However, the police had questioned Gabriella's colleagues at the factory, and had been told she had been wearing a particular necklace that she usually wore. The necklace was not on her person when she was taken to the emergency ward at Frederiksberg hospital, and the police found it on a shelf in the couple's bedroom lying on top of an electric shaver. Blood found on the necklace made the police certain that Istvan had used it to strangle his wife.

Istvan Szabor at the funeral of his wife

Accordingly, at 7pm on Tuesday 28 December, Istvan Szabor was placed under arrest and charged with having strangled his wife, and in court the next day, a magistrate ruled that he had to be kept in custody for four weeks.

A post-mortem was performed on Gabriella but this proved to be inconclusive. The pathologists could not state with certainty what the cause of death had been. They could only say that she had been subjected to various types of violence, but were unable to prove that these had been inflicted on the victim by her husband.

Istvan's suggestion that Gabriella had committed suicide was demolished when Frederiksberg police received a letter from Gabriella's mother in Hungary. In this letter, the mother detailed Gabriella's unhappiness with her marriage in the countless letters she had sent to her mother, citing the main cause of her unhappiness to be Istvan's drunkenness and violence. The mother told police she was absolutely certain her daughter had been killed by Istvan Szabor, who was also after the trade union life insurance of 28,000 kroner.

It was not until 7 October 1977, almost ten months since Gabriella had died, that Frederiksberg police received the final autopsy report. This stated, amongst other findings, that Gabriella had died from strangulation and shock. She had been half-strangled by the necklace she usually wore, and the shock of not being able to breathe had caused her heart to stop.

In court, her husband admitted that they had a fight on her return from work on 27 December, but insisted that it was Gabriella who had assaulted him first, causing him to hit her with a cup on the head. He never confessed that he had, even accidently, squeezed the necklace tightly around her neck causing her death. This was one of the reasons why the police were forced to drop the manslaughter charge, changing it to 'violence causing death'.

In February 1978, Istvan Szabor was sentenced to a mere three years imprisonment in a court in Copenhagen for using severe violence that caused Gabriella's death. His most severe punishment, perhaps, was the fact that his entitlement to Gabriella's 28,000 kroner life insurance payout was denied by the court, which awarded it to her mother in Hungary.

Note: CISS is now known as the International Committee for Deaf Sports (ICSD)

Chapter 5:

The 27-year Cold Case
Chicago, USA 1981-2008

One cold Sunday afternoon in March 1981, two fishermen packing up after a day's fishing at the lake in the Horsetail Slough Forest Preserve in Palos Township, south of Chicago made a "catch" they never expected when they stumbled upon the body of a fully-clothed female among the reeds that surrounded parts of the lake. Detectives who were called out to the scene taped off the area and proceeded to process the scene after it became apparent that the girl had multiple stab wounds.

Horsetail Slough and the lake where the girl's body was found

Other officers pored over Missing persons reports and identified a possible connection with a fifteen-year-old girl reported missing late Wednesday 17 March 1981, and asked the girl's stepfather, Charles L. McCullough, to come to the mortuary and identify the dead body.

Later that evening, a police spokesperson confirmed that the body found at Horsetail Slough was that of fifteen-year-old Dawn Niles, a Deaf freshman student at Hinsdale South High School, Darien, South Chicago, which had a number of Deaf students on the school roll.

A beautiful strawberry-blonde, Dawn Niles had been last seen getting into her boyfriend's car and leaving the school campus with him. Gary Albert was an 18-year-old senior at the same school, and also Deaf.

Dawn Niles was last seen on the Wednesday afternoon 17 March 1981 leaving this school in a car driven by Gary Albert

An autopsy showed that the girl was three-months pregnant with Albert the father, and had been stabbed in a frenzied attack more than 30 times in and around her torso. Unfortunately for the police, Gary Albert's father got him a lawyer before they could question him, and refused the police access to the suspect, and without any other evidence to link him to the murder, the police were forced to shelve the case, much to the disgust of the victim's family and friends.

Over the years, the family of Dawn Niles, particularly her sister, Heather Hunziker, tried to investigate the murder on their own and tried to encourage police to renew the investigation, but were unsuccessful. Once again, they were blocked by lawyers engaged by the Albert family.

The breakthrough came as a result of a totally unrelated criminal offence in which Gary Albert was arrested on misdemeanour charges for secretly filming his 12-year-old stepdaughter in the bathroom of the home he shared with his wife, the mother of the girl. The mother and daughter found a cord in the girl's bathroom which led through a wall and into the attic where there was a television, a video-recorder and videotape that showed the girl getting out of the shower. She was naked in the shots.

This was one occasion where presumably Albert could not rely on his father's lawyers to bail him out and in April 2005, he pleaded guilty to the misdemeanour charge and was placed on a form of probation. His wife started divorce proceedings immediately afterwards, and obtained an order of protection. She, together with her daughter, also filed a lawsuit in 2006 against Albert for the incident, which still has not yet come to court.

The incident, however, caused a former school-mate of Albert and Niles to contact the police by letter as a result of which the police re-opened the investigation. They did this by conducting several witness interviews and the use of technology that was unavailable in 1981 (DNA testing).

By 3 March 2008, the police's cold case squad had made sufficient progress as to feel confident they would make the charges stick, and moved to arrest Gary Albert at the home he was then living at. They arrived just in time, as he was about to run errands and brought him in on charges of first-degree murder. He was up immediately against Judge Raymond Jagielski at the Bridgeview courthouse, and sent to Cook County Jail on a $1 million bond.

The news of Gary Albert's arrest for the murder of Dawn Niles caused a sensation in the Chicago Deaf community

The news of the arrest of Gary Albert spread like wildfire far and wide across America, thanks to website blogs, many of which posted website links so that others could click onto them and follow the case. Many of the comments on these website blogs said things like:

"My blackberry went off like crazy from all my friends telling me did you see the newspaper today? They finally arrested him for the murder of Dawn Niles. I had to get out of bed as fast as I can...Arrested him? Who is him?...As you know the name is already stamped in the back of my head since day one of 22 March 1981 when they found the body... Then I saw the name (in the news). Damn it and I knew it was him all along. What goes round comes round... One thing I have to remember is he is still innocented until proven guilty."

"A beautiful girl, Dawn is resting in peace now. Gary deserve his jail time!!!"

"If Gary did murdered Dawn, I do hope justice will be served to him, let's hope he admits doing this terrible deed. I wonder if it wasn't for DNA technology, would Gary ever admit to murdering the mother of his unborn child, he sure has gotten away with it for 27 years!!! Let's all hope justice will come thru this time without any screw-ups for Dawn Niles and her baby."

But in a blow to everyone, especially the family, Gary Albert was walking about free less than two weeks after his arrest. He got out of Cook County Jail through his father putting up bail of $100,000 (as in most felony cases, bail was set at 10% of the $1 million bond.)

"I feel awful," said Niles' sister Heather Hunziker. She was not the only one. When the author spoke with an ex-classmate recently, it was suggested bitterly that the father and his lawyer would manipulate the justice system for as long as they could so that Gary Albert remained free.

Predictably, Gary Albert's lawyers refused to comment other than to say that he was innocent.

It was clear when the author saw Heather Hunziker during his research in Chicago during September 2009 that she still found the case painful and difficult to talk about.

At the time of writing, Gary Albert has still not come to trial and must be presumed innocent until he is found guilty by any court.

Chapter 6:

Jealousy led to a bloody murder!
Sydney, Australia 1987

When two Deaf people of opposite sexes were allocated flats in a community housing project in Pyrmont Bridge Road, Glebe, Sydney, it was natural that they would associate together for ease of and access to sign language communication. Problems start to arise when one person starts to develop feelings for the other which are not reciprocated even though other Deaf people may label them boyfriend-girlfriend.

Pauline O'Brien, aged 21, had come to Sydney from another part of Australia and needed somewhere to live while she got a job and settled down, whereas Geoffrey Robert Cottle, also 21 years of age, had been a boarder at the New South Wales School for the Deaf at North Rocks, Sydney and did not want to return home to his parents in rural New South Wales.

After living in the community housing project for a few months, Cottle and O'Brien started to go out together before O'Brien began to feel suffocated by the attentions of Geoffrey Cottle and tried to tell him to ease off. When this gentle hint did not work, Pauline O'Brien told Cottle that she did not wish to go out with him anymore, although she would remain friends if he so wished. Cottle did not like what he was being told – he had thought his feelings for

Pauline O'Brien were the same as she had for him, but obviously he was mistaken.

The Royal Institute for the Deaf and the Blind at North Rocks, Sydney, where Geoffrey Cottle went to school.

Being dumped was something that Geoffrey Cottle could not accept, and resentment built up inside him until one Sunday night in February 1987, this resentment boiled over, and Cottle exploded after forcing his way into O'Brien's flat. In a frenzy, Cottle stabbed the girl many times, with blood being splattered everywhere. Such was the ferocity of the attack, particularly on the head and on the face, that O'Brien's features became unrecognisable.

When his frenzy had exhausted itself, Cottle looked around the gory scene in the flat, with the walls and floors all covered in blood, and was appalled. He fled the scene, and cleaned himself up, then went out on his motorbike. Meanwhile, Pauline O'Brien's body was discovered by friends who called at her flat and Geoffrey Cottle became an obvious suspect because of his known relationship with the victim, and was arrested later Sunday night.

Deaf-mute on murder charge

A 21-year-old man appeared in Balmain Local Court yesterday charged with the murder of a deaf-mute woman in Glebe on Sunday night.

Geoffrey Robert Cottle, of Lewisham, is accused of murdering Pauline O'Brien, 21, at her flat in Pyrmont Bridge Road.

The police prosecutor, Mr Martin Blandy, said that Cottle, also a deaf-mute, was arrested after allegedly admitting he had fabricated an earlier story accusing a bikie of the murder.

Bail was refused and Cottle was remanded in custody.

Article from *The Sydney Morning* Herald announcing the arrest.

Cottle was brought before magistrates at Balmain Local Court on Monday 23 February 1987 charged with the murder of Pauline O'Brien. The police prosecutor told the court that Cottle had fabricated a story accusing another biker of the murder before admitting the killing. Bail was refused, and he was remanded in custody to Glebe Coroner's Court on March 4th.

Cottle remained in custody at the Long Bay Penitentiary for several months whilst he was being evaluated and waiting for his trial to take place. Cottle shared his cell with another Deaf person, who was 22 years of age and whom he had known outside the prison system, a policy of fraternisation that was positively encouraged by the NSW Corrective Services Department as a way of providing support and communication to each other.

"People in prison are just like kids on the street or at school," a prison spokesman said. "They need the support of like people, and we try to keep people of similar backgrounds, ages and disabilities together."

On 18 October 1987, before Geoffrey Cottle had appeared in court for his trial, the cellmate found him dead in the cell they shared. Cottle was hanging by two belts attached to the window bars.

The prison authorities said there were no suspicious circumstances, and Cottle had left a note admitting his guilt and saying how sorry he was for killing Pauline O'Brien.

Chapter 7:

The Burnt Body
Bordeaux, France 2001

On early Saturday morning 24 March 2001, firefighters in the city of Bordeaux, south-west France, responded to emergency calls from residents of an apartment block just off the Rue du President Wilson. Flames and thick smoke were coming from the underground garage belonging to the apartment block.

When the firefighters has doused the flames and made safe the building, they found a badly burnt body of a female under some stairs, and there was a strong odour of gasoline in the garage. Suspecting arson with a view to possible concealment of a body, they contacted the Regional Criminal Investigation Service of Bordeaux who sent along a team of detectives plus forensic experts to examine the body. As is customary in France, a magistrate from the Bordeaux Judiciary Service also attended.

The detectives did a door-to-door investigation of the apartment block, seeking to identify if the body belonged to anyone from the building. On the fifth floor, they could get no answer from an apartment rented by a young female. People from neighbouring flats said that a party attended by about 6 people had been going on two nights previously and the young resident of the apartment had not been seen since that party.

The concierge of the apartment block was summoned, and asked to open up the apartment for the detectives, using his master keys, and when the detectives gained access to the apartment, they found a struggle had evidently taken place in the lounge. There were blood splatters all over the walls, and bloodied footprints on the floor.

The autopsy on the body of the badly burnt woman identified her as Dominique Gasse, a 21-year-old Deaf student who attended the institution for the deaf, the Institution Régionale des Sourds et des Aveugles not far away at the Rue Marseilles. The autopsy also found that the cause of death had been blunt trauma to the head. There were several blows that fractured the skull. In addition, the pathologist discovered that the victim had been stabbed 31 times, mostly in the liver, spleen and stomach which had been ripped open and it appeared that the assault with the knife had been particularly ferocious and messy, and the assailant must have been covered with blood.

Two views of the Institution Regionale des Sourds et des Aveugles (Deaf and Blind) at Bordeaux

Back at the apartment, the police realised that there were actually two different sets of footprints in the apartment, meaning that there had been two people there after the death of Dominique Gasse. It also appeared that one of the two people had been in the apartment at least 24 hours after Dominique had been killed, so who was he and what had he been doing in the apartment?

First priority for the police was to trace the people who had been at the party in the apartment. From questioning other residents of the apartment building, it transpired that most of the 6 guests had come to Bordeaux from Paris and were Deaf friends of Dominique from the time she had lived there.

They were all traced, arrested, and then released after it became clear they all had alibis for the time the murders appeared to have taken place. However, some of them informed the police that Dominique had mentioned she was being bothered and hassled for sex by a Deaf Moroccan immigrant. He had not been at the party though.

When the Paris friends gave the police his name, some of them nodded their head sagely. They did not appear surprised, because there had been reports of a Moroccan male hanging around the apartment block. Makdour Hamdi was well-known to the Bordeaux police, who considered him a strong suspect already. They later found his fingerprints inside the apartment which confirmed his involvement.

Aged 22, he had been born in Casablanca and had become deaf at the age of three through meningitis. His mother died a few months afterwards, and Makdour was sent to live with his uncle and aunt in Bordeaux. From that time onwards, he never had any contact with his father or older brother, and indeed with Morocco. In Bordeaux, he went to the same school where later Dominique Gasse would become a student and learnt French Sign Language (LSF).

In his teenage years, he was arrested several times for theft, concealment and acts of violence, mostly against other Deaf people. His last act of violence earned him a short prison sentence. After his release from prison, he started to hang around Dominique Gasse, making it clear he wanted to have sex with her. The psychologists and psychiatrists who examined Hamdi after his last act of violence described him as a wicked person, with psychopathic tendencies due to emotional deprivation. He was basically a homeless person, living in the street or in hostels when not in jail or staying with friends.

Put on the trail of Makdour Hamdi, police found that he had fled Bordeaux. Having reason to believe that he had gone to Paris, Bordeaux police instructed their Paris counterparts to look out for him, which was not really hard because of the colour of his skin and the fact that he could not speak, relying on gestures to communicate with those who did not know LSF, and he was soon apprehended after drawing attention to himself begging in the underground station at Les Halles, the central shopping centre of Paris.

The Les Halles shopping complex in central Paris.
Hamdi was arrested for begging in the underground station below.

Brought back to Bordeaux, he admitted the murder of Dominique Gasse and the subsequent defilement of her body by burning it under the stairs in the underground garage. However, later prior to his arraignment on murder charges he retracted his confession and insisted that the murderer was another Moroccan named Mourad Sadma, aged 21.

At his trial at the Assize Court of the Gironde on Friday 13 June 2003, the court was told that Hamdi had forced his way into the apartment of Dominique Gasse only a matter of minutes after the last of her guests had departed from the party. Dominique had answered the door thinking that one of her guests had returned, perhaps having forgotten something. Instead, she saw Hamdi outside, and despite trying to slam the door on him, he succeeded in getting past her. In the fighting, he had smashed one of the kitchen utensils she was washing up down on her head several times. Once he realised she was probably dead, his frustration at not being able to have sex with her overcame him and he used several of the knives in the kitchen sink to repeatedly stab her about the body.

After washing himself, he made his way out of the apartment unseen, and went to the house of his friend Mourad Souma, who he persuaded to return with him the next night and help to carry the body down to the basement and set it on fire, first having tried to remove as much of the evidence as possible from the apartment.

Makdour Hamdi was sentenced by the jury to a thirty-year term in prison, to the surprise of the Attorney General who had requested 15-20 years. The heavy sentence was partly due to the fact that murder had been extremely brutal and also in recognition of his past record of violence. For his part in "disguising and concealing traces of the murder and tampering with evidence", Mourad Souma was sentenced to five years in prison.

Chapter 8:

The Body on the Back Porch Decking
Morganton, North Carolina, USA 2004

When police officers in Morganton, North Carolina received a telephone call delivered via a relay telephone service about a possible death, they could not have known that it would be the start of a four-year nightmare for many people, particularly the victim's family.

When the first officers arrived at the apartment at 709 West Union Street on Saturday afternoon 8 May 2004, they were met at the door by a man in his mid-thirties who stuck his hands out immediately to be handcuffed. This was ominous and made worse by a powerful odour wafting out through the open front door, the odour of a decomposing body. A quick search revealed a body on the decking outside the back porch, with its torso wrapped in blankets and plastic trash bags. The crime scene was sealed, and forensic scientists called out.

The man who met the officers at the front door said his name was Christopher Lambert. He said he was Deaf, and was then taken to Morganton police headquarters where he was booked in as a material witness to a murder, but he was not saying much at that stage. Police photographed as evidence the bruises on his neck, and several cuts on his hands and legs, which he said were defensive wounds.

It was clear to police scientists that the body had been left out on the back porch for several days – the odour was that bad.

Removed to the mortuary, an autopsy on the body showed that it had been dead at least four to five days, and had 27 stab wounds, mostly to the front of her body. The fatal wounds were believed to be those at her neck and her chest. There were defensive wounds on the hands, and a couple of wounds on the back where, perhaps, she had tried to turn and run into a bedroom for safety. The body was identified as that of Tallie Marie Antolin, aged 31, a Deaf counsellor at the North Carolina School for the Deaf in Morganton.

The North Carolina School for the Deaf,
Where Tallie Antolin worked as a Dorm Counsellor

Tallie Antolin was originally from Anaheim in California, before moving to Massachusetts in the early 1990s, at one time being a Miss Deaf Massachusetts contestant. She then enrolled in Gallaudet in 1998, graduating in 2003 with a BA in American Sign Language and a Minor in Deaf Studies. After Gallaudet, she moved to Morganton and started work as a Dorm Counsellor with the North Carolina School for the Deaf, working with teenage girls with additional disabilities, whilst still working towards her Master's Degree to become a teacher.

Chris Lambert first met Tallie Antollin at Gallaudet University in Washington, D. C.

Chris Lambert was charged with second degree murder of Tallie Antolin, and sent to be held at the Burke-Catawba District Confinement Facility under a $100,000 bond. His statement that the bruises on his neck and cuts on his hands and legs were defensive wounds were rubbished by police scientists who found that he had tried hang himself using a common telephone cord which broke, causing him to fall and knock over a table and lamp with the lamp bulb causing the cuts to his hands and legs. There was also a broken knife in the bathroom and indications that Lambert had cut his hand on it.

Chris Lambert was up to his eyes in debt caused by his addiction to drugs. A note from a drug dealer was found in the apartment warning Lambert to pay up the $180 he owed, and a check on Tallie Antolin's finances showed that in the week before she had been murdered, considerable sums of money had been withdrawn from her bank account, and her credit card was drawn up to the maximum amount allowed. There were also pawnshop dockets in the apartment; apparently Lambert was pawning Antolin's stuff to get even more money to feed his drug habit.

Police thoughts on the matter were that Tallie Antolin had found out what was happening, perhaps because an attempt by her to make a purchase using her credit card somewhere had resulted in a rejection by the store concerned. Police officers found angry notes in the apartment and on Antolin's computer demanding to know from Lambert what was going on, and this set up a confrontation that led to her murder on Tuesday evening 4 May. Even after her death, Lambert was caught on camera taking money out of Antolin's account at ATMs and was also taped pawning even more of Antolin's personal stuff.

It appeared that Lambert had always had a drugs problem ever since he was at Gallaudet where he was said to have always been borrowing money. At one stage, he went for detox but something went wrong there, and he sued the centre where he was receiving treatment for its poor record in providing interpreters, and not surprisingly, blew all he had won in the lawsuit on more drugs as well as a fancy car.

As part of his drugs dependency, he was always getting fired from several jobs for either lateness, absences or even using drugs in the restrooms at work and getting 'high'. He was also a diabetic, which compounded matters. People could never be sure whether he was injecting himself with insulin, or recreational drugs.

After following Tallie Antolin to Morganton, he 'leeched' on her to feed his cocaine habit, using her place to crash out whenever he had nowhere to stay. However much Antolin tried to break away from him, she could not, mainly because she was reported to have loved him and was manipulated by him.

As a result of the findings from the autopsy, the charge against Chris Lambert was upgraded to that of first-degree murder because of the gruesome nature of the killing.

Because of psychiatric evaluations and constant objections by Chris Lambert's defence attorneys over the admissibility of evidence collected by Morganton police, it took four years for the case to come to trial at the Burke County Court. Eventually, after some hard plea-bargaining, Chris Lambert pleaded guilty to charges of kidnapping Tallie Antolin and of her second-degree murder. He was sentenced to 33 years in prison, less the 4 years already served, in the North Carolina Superior Court, Burke County, on 27 May 2008.

Chapter 9:

A Question of legality of a confession in Sign Language
Michigan, USA 2005

When Robert Adelsburg failed to turn up at her house at 4 pm on Friday 22 April 2005 to exercise his court-granted visitation rights with his children, his former wife Kelly Adelsburg was annoyed. It was bad enough having to go through a custody battle over the children, but then just not turn up was unfair on herself and the children, daughter Magen Ann and son Dakota Lee, who were very much looking forward to seeing their father once again.

As the hours passed, Kelly Adelsburg's annoyance became one of concern, especially as Robert failed to answer calls on his TTY (deaf telephone system) or his cellphone, so she put in a call to Robert's mother, Kay, who lived in the same town as Robert.

Kay Adelsburg's attempts to contact her son were also unsuccessful, and she became concerned too. Whatever the differences between Robert and his ex-wife, Kelly, he was a good father who adored his children and it was unheard of for him not to use his visitation rights, and Kelly knew he was looking forward to having them for the weekend.

When Kay told Kelly that she, too, was unable to get a response out of the house in Common Road, Roseville, where Robert lived with his girlfriend of several years, Mary Ann McBride, and that she had also unsuccessfully tried to raise him by text messaging his cellphone, the two women, mother and ex-wife, agreed to meet and go together to the house in Roseville.

Robert Adelsburg

There was something else that was concerning the two women; they were both aware that Robert's relationship with Mary McBride was coming to an end, and he was receiving counselling about ending the relationship.

Robert Adelsburg and Mary McBride had attended different schools for the Deaf. Robert had attended and graduated from the Michigan School for the Deaf at Flint, whilst Mary McBride had gone to the Detroit Day School for the Deaf. They had met through their employment with the US Postal Service, where Robert was a mechanic and Mary was a letter carrier.

In his spare time, Robert liked to help out his friends by repairing any car or motor-cycle problems they had; he also found time to coach the Michigan Deaf School basketball team.

Left: Michigan School for the Deaf;
Right: The MSD basketball team that Robert coached.

It was late at night when the two women arrived at Robert's house, well after 10pm. Lights were on in the house, and Robert's car was still in the driveway, as was Mary's.

When the two women looked through the kitchen door, they spotted what appeared to be blood on the floor and withdrew to call the police out to investigate.

When police officers from Roseville Police Department arrived at 11pm and gained entry to the house, they found blood on the kitchen floor, the landing floor leading to the basement and on the stairway down to the basement. The basement bedroom, where Robert Adelsburg slept, was splattered with blood, and Robert was found dead in a pool of blood on the basement bathroom floor – he had bled to death from a severed artery in the lower leg just above the ankle.

In another part of the house, police found Mary McBride who had attempted to commit suicide by cutting her wrists. They also recovered a blood-stained wooden-handled kitchen butcher's knife.

After Mary McBride was removed to the University of Michigan Hospital for treatment, scene of crimes detectives went all over the crime scene, and theorised that Robert Adelsburg was stabbed while asleep in bed after his night shift, and suffered his fatal wounds whilst trying to escape from Mary.

This theory was confirmed at a subsequent interview with Mary at the Roseville police precinct. Using a sign language interpreter, Detective Sergeant Jon Sarrach elicited information that Mary McBride knew her relationship with the deceased was coming to an end, and that she had stabbed him while he was asleep in bed. He had kicked out at her upon being woken up and tried to escape, and in the process, his leg was slashed, and blood had spurted out.

The interview was videotaped, and in the video, Detective Sarrach was seen to be holding a typed text card containing the Miranda rights, a copy of which was handed over to the accused. At the same time, Sarrach recited the Miranda rights from the card and having his recitation interpreted by the interpreter.

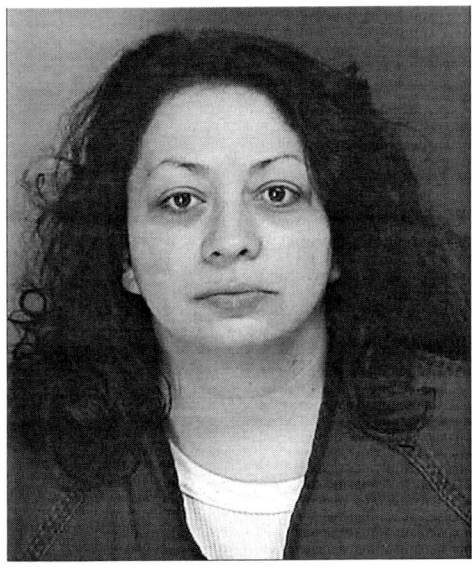

Mary Ann McBride

After this interview, Mary McBride was formally charged with open murder of Robert Adelsburg (meaning that the prosecution had not yet determined what level of homicide to seek against her), and sent to be held in Macomb County Jail without bond. District Court Judge Catherine Steenland scheduled a preliminary examination for May 4th, two weeks hence.

And that should have been that, a very straightforward murder investigation and court case, with an accused caught bang to rights at the crime scene and a confession secured during a video-taped interview.

Only, it didn't work out like that.

In fact, the case descended into legal and constitutional farce when the Macomb County Circuit Court judge, Peter Maceroni, threw out Mary McBride's confession twice.

The crux of the matter was that whilst the videotape showed that Mary McBride had read the typed text on the card given to her in full, it also showed that Detective Sergeant Sarrach had not recited the Miranda rights in full from his card, and these rights had not been interpreted in full by the interpreter.

The defence attorneys argued that this proved the police had failed to adequately communicate certain rights to her, including phrases that advised her of her right to remain silent and request an attorney, whilst the prosecution argued that she could read and write and was seen reading the typed card. Irrelevant, argued the defence attorneys – the fact that Mary McBride could read and write did not mean that she understood her Miranda rights. Also, it was a well-known fact that Deaf people could not read text and watch people signing at the same time and Mary McBride had her head down reading the text during parts of the signed interpretation, which meant she was not following the proceedings in court.

The Macomb County Court where there was a three-year battle over the validity of the "confession" signed by Mary McBride, and how an interpreter communicated to the defendant her Miranda Rights. The case almost became a question of interpreting competence rather than a question of whether Mary McBride was guilty!

The prosecution appealed to the State Supreme Court after the first nixing of the defendant's confession and the Supreme Court found in favour of the prosecution, that police detectives had properly recited McBride's Miranda rights to her, but Judge Maceroni tossed the confession for the second time in October 2008 after four expert witnesses, including two of the prosecution's own witnesses, agreed during an evidentiary hearing that the interpreter had failed adequately to communicate the Miranda rights to Mary McBride.

Defense Attorney Daniel Garon had this to say in a statement outside the court buildings: "An interpreter was there at McBride's interview, but the interpreter did less than an adequate job of communicating the rights to her that the police explained to her. Judge Maceroni said there was no way Mary Anne McBride could reasonably understand what was being explained to her. The interpreter has to make sure that the person understands what they mean."

This public statement, which could have national ramifications on how police deal with deaf defendants, brought forth several angry responses from other interpreters in a website blog:

From a Concerned Interpreter:
"I would just like to comment on one of the statements made by Garon...As a sign language interpreter, it is not our job to make sure the Deaf person understands what is

being said. An interpreter's job is to facilitate communication between hearing and Deaf individuals, and to be a cultural mediator when needed. As interpreters, we can also only interpret to the Deaf person what is spoken by the hearing person, and what the Deaf person signs back to the hearing person. We are forbidden to add any of our own opinions, knowledge or advice. If the Deaf person doesn't understand, it is their responsibility to speak up and say so. As hearing people, if we don't understand what is being explained to us, we have to speak up and say so, why should Deaf people be held to any other standard?"

From a Michigan Interpreter:
"I do not understand why interpreters are now expected to do other people's jobs for them by making sure the deaf person understands what is being said. Shouldn't that be the responsibility of the person saying it?"

From an interested observer:
"This is a dangerous precedent but so typical of many defence attorneys nowadays trying to re-write justice procedures from a Deaf defendant's competency issues to translation issues by interpreters."

From someone calling him or herself Equal Access:
"Deaf people should have the same rights as their hearing peers yet it sounds to me as if they have given McBride more rights by saying the interpreter should have made sure she understood. The Deaf woman in this case should have the same information and rights as any other person

should have. The responsibility shouldn't be put on the interpreter but on the police officer. He probably doesn't explain Miranda in full to hearing people either or make sure they understand clearly all the concepts. Do hearing people understand all the jargon in the Miranda? I guess Deaf people have the same right to get away with murder just as hearing people do, only hearing people don't have an interpreter to blame!"

From Deaf Rights:
It is my understanding the police officer didn't read all the Miranda rights or didn't fully read the Miranda rights to the Deaf person. How is it now the interpreter's fault? Is it the interpreter's fault that someone is afraid to blame the policeman for not doing his job correctly? Why do interpreters have to make sure that the police do their job correctly by checking up on them and ensuring they fully read the Miranda rights then make sure they explain it so the Deaf person understands? What exactly is the job of the police officer then? I don't think this type of liability should be placed on the interpreter. It should be placed on the person who is supposed to accept liability for doing a lousy job or a good job. In this case, the policeman did a lousy job and he is getting away with it because someone decided to blame the interpreter for simply doing their job, interpret what is said, no more, no less."

There were more web-blogs in this vein, most criticising the public statement, but the outcome for the prosecution was that they could not proceed with the case against McBride based on her confession, although there was other evidence that could secure a conviction, though perhaps not of first-degree murder. Judge Maceroni pointed this out when he tossed out the confession for the second time, and set a new pre-trial date in which Mary McBride could either plead guilty or no contest, to a charge lower than first degree murder or decide to proceed to a trial date, with all the risks that the case would fail because of the invalid confession, thus putting the onus on the prosecution to come to a potential plea deal with the defence.

It was the equivalent of asking the prosecution to proceed with one hand tied behind their backs!

So, when the case came to trial in Macomb County Circuit Court in January 2009, it was with the agreement that Mary Anne McBride would plead no contest to the second-degree murder of Robert Adelsburg, and Judge Maceroni sentenced her to 20 to 40 years in prison.

The sentence did not really satisfy the family of Robert Adelsburg. They would have preferred to see a life sentence, but the fact that McBride would have to serve 20 years, less the time she had spent in the Macomb County Jail awaiting trial, went some way towards mollifying them.

Mary McBride would be eligible for parole in slightly less than 16 years from the date of sentencing, with allowances made for the 1400 days that she had already served in the county jail.

Mary Ann McBride when Judge Maceroni's sentence was read out to her

Chapter 10:

Cut Up and Scattered on a Landfill Site
Poland 2005

A collector scavenging for scrap on a landfill site near the town of Slawno in north-west Poland got the shock of his life when he opened a black plastic bag and discovered a human arm. After throwing up his breakfast, the scrap collector called the police.

The first officials on the scene in the afternoon of 23 June 2005 took one look and decided it was a matter for the homicide detective squad based in the city of Koszalin, the administrative centre of that part of the province of Zachodniopomorskie, which was about 42 kilometres from Slawno.

The detectives from Koszalin viewed the landfill site with great distaste, and suitably attired in preventive clothing, reluctantly started searching for the rest of the body. From the texture of the skin on the arm, which had been crudely cut away from the rest of the body, the chief forensic scientist at the scene hazarded a guess that they would be looking for a young woman. He also said that the arm had not been there very long, perhaps less than 24 hours.

By the end of the day, more plastic bags containing body parts had been found. Other police officers searching a row of dustbins in a garbage disposal facility near the landfill site found more plastic bags.

In the mortuary, the body parts were re-assembled as best as the pathologist could, and it was confirmed that the body was that of a young woman, possibly a teenage girl. She had apparently been viciously stabbed a number of

Newspaper article dated 27 June 2005 showing the landfill site where some of the body parts were discovered, together with a picture of the victim

times before her body was dismembered and packed in plastic bags and either thrown onto the landfill site or placed in several dustbins.

Police enquiries in and around Slawno revealed that a young Deaf girl named Martyna Bielska had not been seen for a few days, although she had not yet been reported missing. Aged only 17, Martyna was the girlfriend of a Deaf man named Robert Lewandowski, aged 21, who was a trainee chef.

Article from newspaper dated 27 June 2005 with the scavenger indicating where he found some of the body parts

After he was brought in for questioning, and while waiting for a sign language interpreter, police officers obtained a warrant to search his home where they discovered a quantity of marijuana. This gave the police the opportunity to hold onto Lewandowski while they pursued their enquiries. It was evident, however, that the killing and dismemberment of Martyna Bielska had not taken place in Lewandowski's home. Robert Lewandowski himself flatly denied he had anything to do with the murder of his girlfriend.

Further enquiries brought to light the fact that Lewandowski was friends with another Deaf man who also lived in Slawno, 31-year-old Marek Sydoruk, who was arrested when forensic evidence showed that there had been large quantities of blood spilled in his flat. This blood proved to belong to Martyna Bielska.

Marek Sydoruk

Under questioning, Sydoruk owned up to having the girl killed in his flat, but told police that Lewandowski had been the one who had stabbed the girl, and he (Sydoruk) had merely helped Lewandowski to cut up and dispose of the body.

Lewandowski protested that he had been at work at the time the murder was supposed to have taken place, and this was confirmed by other employees at the restaurant where he was trainee chef. Despite this, Lewandowski was arrested for the murder of his girlfriend along with Sydoruk and both men were charged on 27 June 2005. Lewandowski's protests were not helped by the discovery by police, who had seized his computers, that he had been systematically pirating computer software programs. Also, one of Martyna's friends was accusing him of attempted rape.

Robert Lewandowski
entering court

In the first court session following the arrest, Marek Sydoruk admitted that he alone was responsible for the killing of Martyna Bielska in his flat, and that Lewandowski had not been involved in any way. Sydoruk told the court through a sign language interpreter that he had lost his temper after the teenage girl had taunted him over his sexual preferences, calling him a pervert. He had hit out at the girl, and when he had recovered his senses, she was dead. In a panic, he had cut up her body, causing blood to be spilled all over his flat and disposing them in the dustbins and also on the landfill site.

As the landfill site was popular with scrap scavengers, he had to do the disposal in the dark to avoid being seen, and this meant that the bags were not as well disposed of as they might have been.

This changed testimony was not enough to have Robert Lewandowski released, and he remained in custody without bail for the next two years whilst the prosecutors' office made preparations for the trial in the District Court in Koszalin.

Robert Lewandowski, and behind him, Marek Sydoruk, in court behind glass screens.

When the court convened in November 2007, the trial judge Robert Maka made an order that the proceedings would be conducted in camera on account of the explicit nature of the crime and the necessity to bring up details of the sexual life of the accused, which were therefore never publically revealed. It is believed, however, that these related to paedophilia practices.

Judge Maka ruled, however, that the final speeches, the sentence and its justification would be open to the public. In the sentencing phase, he said that Marek Sydoruk would be imprisoned for 25 years, but would be able to apply for parole after 20 years.

The judge justified this sentence on the grounds that all the evidence presented to the court led to the logical conclusion that only Marek Sydoruk was responsible for the crime of murdering Martyna Bielska. It was accepted that the murder had not been premeditated, and had only taken place because the victim had mercilessly mocked Sydoruk's sexual preferences, causing him to lose control. The fact that the accused had gone to the trouble of dismembering the body in an effort to conceal the murder added weight to the severity of the sentence.

Robert Lewandowski, acquitted of murder, awaits his sentence for drugs offences and computer puiracy.

As for Robert Lewandowski, the court accepted that he had not been involved in the murder, and of this, he was acquitted. However, Judge Maka found it had been proved that Lewandowski had (a) been in possession of marijuana (b) been involved in computer software piracy (c) issued threats to a friend of Martyna Bielska that he would rape her. For these offences, Lewandowski was sentenced to three years imprisonment. As he had already spent 2½ years in custody waiting for the trial, it was decided this was sufficient punishment and Lewandowski was freed immediately.

Chapter 11:

A shotgun settles an argument
Pennsylvania, USA 2005

Thomas Simich, Sr. and his wife Dorothy were getting on in years. Thomas was 80 years-old and Dorothy was 83 years-old, and they had lived in their house at 239½ Fifth Avenue, Freedom, Pennsylvania for well over 50 years ever since they got married. However, they were now finding the steep steps at the front of the house a real problem for their aged and creaky joints. An offer to move into special assisted living accommodation for the elderly seemed a very attractive proposition, but this meant they had to sell the house they had lived in all their married life.

The main stumbling block to selling the house was the presence of their son, Thomas, Jr. He had been living with his parents ever since his marriage to a girl he had known in school was dissolved in 1986.

Although the parents were both Deaf and used colloquial American Sign Language, they were having a bit of a problem communicating the idea of selling their house to Thomas Junior, who was also Deaf.

They asked their friends in the senior citizens group that met regularly at the Western Pennsylvania School for the Deaf about 15 miles from their home in Edgewood, Pittsburgh what they ought to do. The consensus was that it might be better to ask their Deaf daughter and Deaf son-in-law to come up from Florida where they now lived, and try and explain things to Thomas, Jr. All the Simichs, including their cousins the Hudocks, went to the Western Pennsylvania School, therefore the family was very well known in the small town of Freedom (population 1,800) and around Pittsburgh. Thomas Jr. had been great mates with his brother-in-law while they were at school, and all three of them had grown up together until the sister and brother-in-law moved down to Florida.

The Simichs' daughter, Marilyn Bergman and her husband Steven Bergman, thought it would be a good idea to come up and see their parents and try to explain things to Thomas, Jr., who was now having some mental health problems and finding certain things difficult to grasp. The Bergmans left their four Deaf children with their paternal

Marilyn and Steven Bergman

grandparents, who lived near them in Palm Bay, Florida, and drove to the Simich home in Freedom, arriving there on late Friday 30 April.

After a pleasant weekend together, Marilyn and Steven Bergman now broached the thorny subject of the sale of their parents' house so that they could move into an assisted living facility. No-one knows what really happened next, not even the aged parents, but Thomas, Jr. lost his cool, ranting and raving that they were all trying to force him out of the home that was his by birthright.

As his sister and brother-in-law tried to pacify him, Thomas, Jr. snatched up a shotgun and started waving it round. As Thomas, Sr. and Dorothy Bergman watched aghast, Steven Bergman threw himself across his wife to shield her but was too late. Thomas Simich Jr. fired the shotgun at point blank range into the back of his sister's neck, and Marilyn Bergman's blood spattered all over her father's shirt and face. As Thomas Jr. continued to wave the gun round, Steven Bergman's next thought was to draw fire away from the elderly parents, and he moved towards the door but did not make it. Another shotgun blast downed him.

As there were no more shells in the shotgun, Thomas Sr. grabbed it from him and quickly ushered his frail wife out of the room, out of the house and down the steps and hurried her towards some neighbours who had come out of their houses to see what the shooting was about.

When the paramedics arrived in response to a 9-1-1 call from one of the neighbours, they found Steven Bergman's body at the front of the house, with blood running down the steps that had been the original problem leading to the proposed sale. They found Marilyn Bergman inside, still breathing, and rushed her to Beaver Medical Center but she died shortly afterwards.

Steven Bergman's body being removed by paramedics from the house.

The first police officers to arrive from Rochester were unaware that the shooter still inside the house was deaf and tried to communicate with Thomas Simich Jr. by loudspeaker and by telephone, until they were put right by neighbours. They then called out a sign language interpreter from the Center for Hearing and Deaf Services in Pittsburgh and stayed outside, making no attempt to get into the house.

When Thomas Simich looked out of the window and saw the interpreter, he came outside and surrendered quietly without incident.

Thomas Simich Jr. being led from the house after his arrest.

Marilyn Bergman, who ran her own business in Palm Bay and West Melbourne, Florida called Marilyn's Superior Cleaning Service, and Steven Bergman, a retired postal clerk, would have celebrated their 25th wedding anniversary in less than a month. Because of the difficulties in communication between Pennsylvania and Florida, Rochester police requested that Palm Bay police contact the family, preferably through the paternal grandparents who were also Deaf, and ask them to explain the tragic circumstances to their grandchildren, two of whom were still at school in St. Augustine at the Florida School for the Blind and Deaf, some 250 miles up the coast.

When Thomas Simich Jr. was arraigned for the shooting, it was evident that he was suffering from severe mental health problems and Judge John McBride of the Beaver County Circuit Court made an order that Simich was to undergo a psychiatric examination.

When Simich appeared before court again on 6 October 2005, Dr. Christine Martone, a forensic psychiatrist experienced in evaluating criminal defendants, told the court that she attributed his behaviour to paranoid schizophrenia. She said that Simich, who was abusing cocaine, told her he was having voices speaking in his head. He thought Marilyn and Steven Bergman belonged to a cocaine cartel and that he was a federal narcotics agent sent to arrest them.

Richard Hudock, a Deaf cousin and a regular childhood playmate of Simich, told the court that he had noticed Tommy (as Simich was known in the neighbourhood) had been "slipping" for a few months before the shooting occurred and had decided it was probably not a good idea to have him around his children.

"He was talking to somebody who wasn't there. The guy that you see there *(in the court)* is definitely not the same person I used to know."

Judge John McBride referred him to Mayview State Hospital for 90 days for further evaluations to be made on his competency to stand trial.

Mayview State Hospital before its closure in December 2008

At the time of writing (January 2010) Thomas Simich Jr. still has not come to trial. He was still in Mayview State Hospital when that hospital closed for good on 28 December 2008. By law, Thomas Simich has to be periodically evaluated so that court officials know whether his status has changed and he is competent to stand trial. At present, this seems highly unlikely, and because he needs supervised care, he was not moved into the Rolling Hills Assisted Living Center in Baldwin Township with most of the former patients in Mayview, but was transferred to the Torrance State Hospital in Westmoreland County.

Chapter 12:

The Sioux Falls Chainsaw Murder
South Dakota, USA 2006

When colleagues and managers of JDS Industries, a company in Sioux Falls, South Dakota specialising with the manufacture and import of trophies, awards and plaques, found that one of their employees had not turned up for work two days in a row on 2 and 3 February 2006, the management decided to find out what was wrong.

The employee, bubbly but overweight Darlene VanderGiesen, was normally very dependable, having worked for over a decade on one of the company's checking and packing stations preparing products for dispatch, and it was most unlike her not to call in if she was sick. Being Deaf, 42-year-old VanderGiesen was also very popular amongst the company's employees, many of whom had learnt ASL in order to communicate with her.

When colleagues sent to her apartment to check on the absent employee could not get an answer at the door, or from the TTY or cellphone, the company contacted her parents in Iowa with their concerns and learnt that they had had no contact either, and no-one could be found who had seen her since she left her employer's parking lot at 6 pm on Wednesday 1 February. The disappearance was reported to the Sioux Falls police department, who soon found the missing woman's car late Friday evening in a Pizza Hut parking lot.

When Darlene's parents arrived in Sioux Falls from Iowa to help in the search, they let themselves into their daughter's home and found her cats hungry. They also found that she had left her cellphone behind. This led them to believe that their daughter had not simply run off, because she relied so much on the cellphone, using it for text messages.

 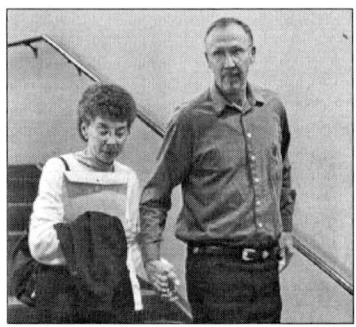

Left: Darlene VanderGiesen with one of her cats, and *right:* her parents who came to look for her and report her as missing.

In a missing persons report circulated by the Sioux Falls police department, Darlene VanderGiesen was described as five foot five in height, between 200 and 250 pounds with brown hair and hazel eyes, and in her 40s.

Questioning employees at the Pizza Hut restaurant, it was soon established that the missing woman had been seen eating with another Deaf female during the early part of the evening. The female was described as being in her 40s as well, and was an African-American.

Over the weekend, through examining the computer in the missing woman's flat and checking emails, some of which in the name of "Wendy Smith" containing insulting messages, police found other emails from an ex-boyfriend in Iowa but were soon able to eliminate him. Through other emails, police were able to focus on a woman named Daphne Wright, who matched the description of the woman seen with Darlene VanderGiesen in the Pizza Hut restaurant.

Initially, Daphne Wright denied that she had been with Darlene VanderGiesen in the Pizza Hut, but confronted with other proof, she soon changed her story and admitted that they had both been there but that the two women had gone their separate ways when they left the restaurant.

However, this lie enabled the police to apply for a search warrant of the home in Sioux Falls that Wright shared with another woman. Although Wright was a lesbian, she was not currently having a relationship with the woman, Jeannette Martin[1], a former lover.

In the execution of the search warrant, police officers discovered pieces of bone, flesh and drops of blood in the basement of the shared home. After this discovery, police asked both women to come down to the local police station for questioning. Later, DNA would link these findings to Darlene VanderGiesen.

---

[1] *Not her real name. No purpose would be served in revealing this.*

Among other things that were taken from the house were computers. Police also removed a computer from Sallie Collins' apartment, and one from the victims. From these computers, forensic IT specialists would find numerous emails between Wright and VanderGiesen, and also Collins and VanderGiesen. Of particular note was an online conversation that Wright had with Sallie Collins on the evening of 1 February, the night that Darlene VanderGiesen disappeared.

The death house, where police found pieces of bone, flesh and blood.

It soon became clear that there were many inconsistencies in Daphne Wright's story. When Martin with told police that she had seen Wright remove a carpet bundle, and other trash in a black bag from the house, police officers knew they were now looking at a murder investigation. It was also telling that Wright had repainted the room, possibly in an attempt to cover up blood marks. The other woman was released from police custody and cautioned that she was now a material witness in the case. At one time, it did look as if police would charge Sallie Collins with complicity in the murder, but in the end decided that Collins was totally innocent and knew nothing about the murder. Later in the trial, it would be a defence ploy to shift blame for the murder onto Collins.

Turning back to Daphne Wright, police officers video-taped the next interview, carried out with the aid of a sign language interpreter, and eventually, Wright admitted that she had kidnapped Darlene VanderGiesen from the Pizza Hut restaurant and brought her to her house where she killed her in a jealous rage because she suspected VanderGiesen was trying to break up her lesbian relationship with another Deaf woman named Sallie Collins in order to have Collins for herself. This did not really make sense because VanderGiesen was an acknowledged heterosexual, and Sallie Collins later told police that she and VanderGiesen were just friends. It was also clear that the relationship between Collins and Wright had run its course, and they were no longer lovers.

As a result of this interview, at least 25 police officers descended upon a landfill site outside Sioux Falls. However, deep snow and bad weather prevented them making a start in searching the site for a few days. In total, it took the police nearly three weeks to complete their fingertip search of the landfill site.

Even then, they never found the upper parts of the body.

Police officers and forensic scientists spent three weeks in extremely cold weather searching the Sioux Falls' landfill site for body parts.

Daphne Wright made her first court appearance on Monday 13 February, handcuffed, and in court did not sign anything but her court-appointed attorney told the judge that Wright would be pleading "not guilty" to the murder of VanderGiesen. Wright was remanded to be held in the Minnehaha County Jail without bond.

Daphne Wright at her first court appearance.

In the meantime, police officers interviewed employees at tool and hardware stores around Sioux Falls in an effort to discover whether Wright had purchased any cutting equipment as the first parts of VanderGiesen body indicated she had been cut up with an electrical tool.

After Darlene VanderGiesen was buried in Rock Valley, Iowa, Daphne Wright was indicted to stand trial for the first-degree murder of VanderGiesen, although there were serious procedural concerns linked with the decision for the trial to go ahead. For instance, it was later established that Daphne Wright's *Miranda Rights* had never been read out or signed to her before either of her interviews.

However, the Sioux Falls deaf community was quite small, having no more than 200 members, and Darlene VanderGiesen was extremely popular and well-liked. On the other hand, Daphne Wright was an outsider, having gone to school at the North Carolina School for the Deaf (from which school, incidentally, she was kicked out of, failing to graduate). She had initially moved into Sioux Falls in the summer of 2000 after she had met Jeanette Martin in Maryland and accepted her invitation to move in with her. When her relationship with Martin ended in 2002, she met up with Sallie Collins who was living in Madison, Wisconsin at the time, and went to live there with her. In 2004, both women accepted an invitation from Martin to move in with her at Sioux Falls. How Martin felt about her ex-lover living with a new lover in her own home is a matter for conjecture.

In any event, all three of them lived together in Martin's house until Collins moved out into her own apartment sometime during the summer of 2005. The reason she gave was that she felt "suffocated" by Daphne Wright and wanted her own circle of friends, both straight and gay, something that Wright, who rarely mixed with the Sioux Falls deaf community, resented. Although Collins and Wright still met up for sex occasionally and Wright continued to regard her as "her girlfriend", Collins used her independence away from Wright to have a more active and balanced social life, and one of the friends she made was Darlene VanderGiesen. There was never any suggestion that Collins and VanderGiesen had any sort of sexual relationship, as imagined by Daphne Wright.

Because of this, many Deaf people wanted the law to come down hard on Daphne Wright, many advocating the death penalty for her. This was also wanted by the Minnehaha County State's Attorney Dave Nelson, despite the fact no-one had been legally executed in South Dakota for over 60 years. To make his case even stronger, Darlene VanderGiesen's upper body parts were found, more than six weeks after the murder had been committed.

Two road maintenance workers were just going about their usual Spring task of filling in winter-ravaged potholes and picking up garbage north of Beaver Creek, Minnesota, which was across the state line from South Dakota, when they stumbled upon human remains wrapped in a blanket in a ditch. A subsequent autopsy proved they were the remains of Darlene VanderGiesen. Even with this find, some body parts were still missing, and the same highway maintenance crew said they had seen a five-gallon bucket about half-a-mile from where they had discovered the body. However, when they went to find it, the bucket was no longer there.

However, a further autopsy of these remains led Minnehaha County State's Attorney Nelson to surmise that

Darlene VanderGiesen was killed by a skull fracture, or suffocation, or both. The body parts were too badly cut up and decomposed to determine the exact cause of death.

One particular problem for both the State and the defence was that Deaf people throughout the United States were following the case avidly on the Internet, many of them volunteering information about Daphne Wright and her relationships with Jeannette Martin and Sallie Collins – information that could not be used at any trial. Also, several of these Deaf Internet bloggers openly advocated the death penalty for Wright, whilst others raised the issue of her having a fair trial because she was Deaf, black and a lesbian.

It took until March/April 2007 for the case to come to trial at the Minnehaha County Circuit Court in Sioux Falls before Circuit Judge Bradley Zell. It would be the first time ever that a female accused would face a capital punishment trial in South Dakota. The delay had been caused by pre-trial hearings to decide on Wright's competency. One defence witness, an expert psychologist on deaf people, testified that it was borderline whether Wright could understand what was going on in the courtroom; he said that Wright read at third-grade level and might not easily grasp the definition of some legal terms, such as Miranda Rights.

"When a deaf person uses the term 'rights', they mean right like to the right hand or right like correct," he told the court, saying that Wright should have access to a CDI (Certified Deaf Interpreter), who would explain to Wright via consecutive interpreting in her own language what was happening.

Minnehaha County Courthouse where the trial took place

However, Judge Zell made a ruling, concluding that Wright could understand very well what was happening in the courtroom, particularly as it was outfitted with projection screens that printed out what everyone was saying. Each question, answer and statement would automatically be displayed on the screens as the court reporter transcribed the proceedings. Judge Zell also pointed out that sign language interpreters would be in the front of the room and next to Wright.

Jury selection was to take an incredible four weeks as both prosecution and defence struggled to get a jury to their liking, and it was not until Monday 2 April 2007 that the trial proper got under way, with Daphne Wright pleading guilty to premeditated first-degree murder of Darlene VanderGiesen.

In his opening statement, lead prosecutor Dave Nelson outlined the evidence he would introduce that would show exactly what the prosecution believed had happened. On the other hand, main defence attorney Traci Smith simply said that Wright did not kidnap VanderGiesen and did not cause her death.

The second day focused upon the videotapes made of Wright's interviews, which told two different stories. The defence sought to exclude these tapes because the conversations had been interpreted and Wright did not fully understand her rights.

At the end of the taped interview, Wright was asked by Detective Michael Olson if there had been an argument in Pizza Hut. Wright denied this, and also stated that VanderGiesen had never been in her SUV. State's Attorney Nelson told jurors that this was a lie, and they would soon hear evidence that a drop of the victim's blood had been found in the vehicle.

One of the points at issue was how Wright had managed to get Darlene VanderGiesen into the SUV to be driven away from the restaurant parking lot, leaving her car there, as VanderGiesen was very heavyset (weighing around 15-16 stone), and VanderGiesen used to be able to look after herself at school, fighting boys.

Daphne Wright during her trial

Not only that, but how also did Wright, who was much lightly-built than her victim, manage to get VanderGiesen out of the SUV at her house at 1806 South Phillips Avenue, Sioux Falls where the driveway was in open view of neighbouring houses, into the house, then down into the basement without Jeannette Martin being aware of it. This is why for a long time police believed she must have had help.

But fingernail scrapings, buccal swabs (taken from inside the cheeks), plucked head and pubic hair and fingerprints taken from Jeannette Martin on 7 February did not reveal any of Darlene VanderGiesen's DNA on them, thus removing her as a suspect. The other possible suspect, Sallie Collins, had an unshakeable alibi for the evening and night in question, although this did not prevent the defence pointing the finger at her as the person responsible for the murder of VanderGiesen.

So in the end, the police and prosecution were forced to believe that Wright had *somehow* managed to do all this by herself.

But Sallie Collins did take the stand in court to testify that she did not see or communicate with Daphne Wright the night police say Wright killed VanderGiesen. However, she did testify that the weekend before the victim disappeared, she and Wright were in Collins' apartment when VanderGiesen turned up unannounced. Wright went mad because she thought VanderGiesen was trying to butt into her relationship with Collins; VanderGiesen made an obscene gesture to Wright and left the apartment. The next day, however, Wright wanted to patch things up, and VanderGiesen came back, and all three appeared to get along for the rest of the weekend. Collins stated that she knew Wright planned to get together with VanderGiesen on the day she disappeared, but when she asked her ex-girlfriend about the meeting, Wright said it never happened. After the disappearance, Collins said she wanted to go over to VanderGiesen's apartment to give support to her family and friends, and took Wright with her, but Wright appeared to be uneasy and wanted to leave after just five minutes, especially after embracing VanderGiesen's mother.

Several jurors looked sick when the gory photographs of the cut-up body were displayed on the screens in court. This was also too much for the victim's parents and sister, who left the courtroom. State's Attorney Nelson said that the photographs would be sealed and never be seen again after the court case as he did not want other outlets gaining access to them.

Minnehaha County Coroner Brad Randall used the photographs to describe what he had learnt about the victim's death and chainsaw dismemberment. That a chainsaw had been used was confirmed by a receipt found in Wright's possession. He said that VanderGiesen had died from suffocation, blunt head trauma or a combination of the two.

Associate defence lawyer Jeff Larson suggested on cross-examination that VanderGiesen could have died from falling down the basement steps and banging her head against a beam. But Randall replied that a seven-inch skull fracture over the right ear, plus heavy bruising on the top, back, left and right sides of the head indicated her death was no accident.

After the state had rested its case on Tuesday 10 April, the defence called seven witnesses in an attempt to prove that it had been another person, not Daphne Wright, who had killed Darlene VanderGiesen. Wright herself was not amongst those called by the defence.

One of the witnesses brought in was a forensic pathologist from another state who provided an alternative opinion of how the victim died in an attempt to support the defence's suggestion that VanderGiesen died accidently by falling down the stairs leading to the basement in Wright's house.

After closing statements from both prosecution and defence, the jury deliberated for seven hours before turning in its guilty verdict just before noon on Thursday 12 April, setting up a possible death sentence for Wright, who cried as she read the verdict on the hands of her ASL interpreter.

Now, the jury had to make a decision on what sort of sentence to hand down to Daphne Wright, and they returned to court on Wednesday 18 April to do this.

This time, after ten hours deliberation, they returned to court at 8:30 p.m. that night to hand down their decision. The foreperson of the jury of 11 women and one man was physically shaking when she informed the court that

Daphne Wright would not die for murdering Darlene VanderGiesen. The jury all felt it was important that they delivered the decision directly to Wright, instead of having the judge do it for them.

Daphne Wright cries as the
verdict is read out in court

"We wanted her to know that we were more merciful to her than she was to Darlene," one of them said afterwards. Out of the twelve jurors, seven had voted for life without parole, with four sitting on the fence, and only one was set on the death penalty. In South Dakota, the decision had to be unanimous only if the verdict was death.

Darlene VanderGiesen's family after the verdict

At the conclusion of the trial, Darlene VanderGiesen's parents read a statement to Daphne Wright, in which they forgave her for murdering their daughter, even though it would leave a big hole in their lives.

Daphne Wright would now spend the rest of her life in the South Dakota Women's Prison in Pierre, where there were five other women serving life without parole. Corrections Department officials admitted there were no other deaf women within the prison, and that none of the staff could use ASL, but they were sure that she would be treated the same as any other inmate within the prison. However, a spokesperson for the American Civil Liberties Union national Prison Project said that Wright's deafness was a disability covered by the federal Americans with Disabilities Act, and that the prison authorities must make reasonable adjustment to provide access to programmes and services, even if this involved providing ASL interpreters. They said the onus was on the Department of Corrections to make sure that this happens.

On 25 March 2009, it was announced that Daphne Wright would appeal her sentence, listing the following as issues leading to grounds for appeal:

1. Whether the trial court abused its discretion in denying Wright's motion to suppress statements made during the interview at the law enforcement centre.

2. Whether the trial court should have granted Wright's request for consecutive interpretation during the trial and provided a CDI, as recommended by the distinguished psychologist and expert on the deaf at one of the pre-trial hearings.

3. Whether the trial court's system of selecting jurors, in which African-Americans were under-represented, violated Wright's constitutional rights.

4. Whether the trial court erred in allowing evidence of a prior altercation concerning Wright, VanderGiesen, and Collins, that took place the weekend before the murder in Collins' apartment.

5. Whether there was sufficient evidence to support the jury's verdicts of felony murder and premeditated murder.

6. Whether Wright's kidnapping conviction violated double jeopardy.

7. Whether cumulative error denied Wright a fair trial.

At the time of writing (January 2010), this appeal has yet to be heard.

Some of the Deaf community around Sioux Falls expressed annoyance that other Deaf people from outside the state of South Dakota are promoting the appeal and supporting Daphne Wright, being what they see as more interested in her rights.

"What about the rights of Darlene VanderGiesen?" they have pointed out, as they establish a memorial in her name.

Chapter 13:

Murder in a Deaf Town
Jacksonville, Illinois, USA 2006

If there is any town in the USA that could be called a typical Deaf town or city, then that place is Jacksonville, Illinois. It has a population of 19,000 and compared to other towns and cities of similar populations, it has a higher ratio of Deaf people to non-deaf people. This is due, chiefly, to the presence of the Illinois School for the Deaf. Established in February 1839, it currently has in excess of 300 children on its pupil roll ranging from a nursery class up to students aged around 19.

Illinois School for the Deaf, Jacksonville

Because of the presence of the school, Deaf people tend to move into the area and subsequently, there is a strong support network for Deaf people within the town. Regular sign language classes are held within the school to enable the townsfolk to acquire ASL (American Sign Language) skills so that they can communicate with local Deaf citizens. There are for example staff within the J C Penny superstore and other stores who are fluent in ASL, and one cannot avoid bumping into other Deaf people while out in the locality. The author and his wife, whilst researching in the area, encountered a car load of Deaf people at a local petrol station, saw several Deaf people in the local shops and a number of shopkeepers and other customer service personnel within stores and restaurants were able to use ASL. Even some local police officers have acquired ASL.

Given the closeness of the local Deaf community, it was no wonder that when a murder of a prominent local Deaf person was discovered, the shock reverberated throughout the town.

It started one morning on Wednesday 22 March 2006 when two little boys aged 7 and 4 went to a Deaf neighbour who lived on the same mobile home park, the Northwood Mobile Home Park. When the neighbour, who had been a classmate and a best friend of the boys' mother, opened the door to the boys, she knew immediately something was very wrong. Leaving the boys in the temporary care of another neighbour, the friend ran to the boys' residence, a mobile home on Stratford Lane, Jacksonville. Upon arrival, she found her friend, Amber Danielle Burroughs, in her bedroom and after failing to get a response, had someone call out the police and the emergency medical services, who subsequently pronounced the woman dead.

Two views of the Stratford Lane block of
Northwood Mobile Home Park.

Initially, police refused to disclose how the death had occurred but later admitted the cause of death had been suffocation. They also announced they were looking for the partner of the dead woman, and father of the two boys, Aaron Winfert, who had been released from the Morgan County Detention Facility only the day previous to the discovery of the murder. He had been held on charges for residential burglary and theft, but had made bail thanks to a social security cheque deposited with the police by, ironically, Amber Burroughs and the friend who found her dead later the same week.

Amber Burroughs was aged 26 at the time of her death. She had been born in Peoria, a town in northern Illinois, and had been educated at the Illinois School for the Deaf, graduating in 1997. She came from a Deaf family and had stayed on in Jacksonville after graduating from the school because of the strong support networks available in the area.

Amber and Aaron Winfert had started associating together whilst still at the school, and although Amber graduated, Aaron did not, dropping out of the school in his final year after committing a number of felonies, which included burglarising the Illinois School for the Deaf's elementary school building in 1997, for which he served a sentence of 97 days and was placed on probation for 4 years. The following year, he served another sentence for the illegal use of a debit card.

Amber Burroughs

Despite his minor criminal history, Amber Burroughs began to live together with Aaron Winfert, and bear his children. The relationship did not meet with general approval from Burrough's family or other Deaf friends. After the birth of her second child, Burroughs began work at the Alvin Eades Center in Jacksonville, which provided residential care and other services for people with multiple disabilities, including deafness.

However, by January 2006, just prior to Winfert's sentencing for residential burglary and theft, Amber

Burroughs had enough of the relationship and sought an order of protection against Aaron Winfert in the Morgan County Circuit Court, which was granted by default when Winfert failed to attend.

In her written request for the court order, Amber Burroughs had alleged that Winfert had pulled a knife on her and threatened to harm her when she asked him to move out of her home because of his use of drugs and for constantly stealing from her and her sons to feed his drugs habit. It was alleged that he had taken and sold his son's Sony Playstation on three separate occasions. The written request detailed Aaron Winfert's long list of felonies, including a 1999 conviction for stealing a Pontiac Grand Am from a Jacksonville car dealership. Also outstanding were two other cases, a 2005 felony for forgery and a misdemeanour for resisting a police officer who was trying to arrest him.

Jacksonville detectives traced Aaron Winfert to his sister's home in Chicago, where he was arrested by local police officers on the Wednesday night on a warrant for violating the order of protection filed by Burroughs. He had used Burroughs's car to get to Chicago. He was brought back to Jacksonville at 5:15 am the next morning by two police officers and Sergeant Joe Tapscott, who served as police interpreter for Jacksonville.

When he appeared in court later that day for his preliminary hearing, Aaron Winfert was charged with three alternate counts of murder to cover possible intentions or states of mind that he might put forward as a defence. However, if convicted, it would be on the single count of first-degree murder that the judge and jury felt was most appropriate to the circumstances.

Aaron Winfert after his arrest

In a relatively short period of less than three months, the case came to trial on Wednesday 7 June 2006 in the Morgan County Circuit Court before Judge Richard Mitchell. The quick time between the murder and the trial was the result of a negotiated plea worked out between Public Defender Tom Piper and the State Attorney, Chris Reif. This involved Aaron Winfert pleading guilty to a first-degree murder charge under the state's Truth in Sentencing law, which meant that Winfert would have to serve every day of the 30-year sentence imposed by Judge Mitchell.

Winfert was also convicted of the various criminal cases pending against him, receiving three years for felony theft, five years for felony forgery and 364 days for resisting a police officer. All sentences were to be run concurrent with the main 30-year term.

Chapter 14

The Fatal Shooting that Ended a 24-Year Relationship, Michigan, USA 2007

When Joseph Catalano was woken up by the arrival of his son, Timothy, in the early hours of Monday 27 August 2007, he knew immediately something was very wrong. The father said later that, "He was livid. He was all upset and everything."

After sitting down his agitated son and calming him down, Joseph Catalano asked what the matter was. He suspected, as usual, that it would be to do with his son's relationship with his long-time girlfriend, Tammy Lee Susalla. The relationship has been showing signs of strain recently. The response was not what Joseph Catalano expected. His son blurted out that he had killed Tammy Lee, and had left her body in the house that they shared at Gloria Street, Westland, Wayne County, Michigan.

Timothy Catalano and Tammy Lee Susalla had been high school sweethearts at Detroit Day School for the Deaf, and had lived together for 24 years, 19 of them in the same house at Westland, but the father had witnessed recently the badly deteriorating relationship between his son and Tammy Lee, with a history of domestic violence.

With a heavy heart, Joseph Catalano contacted the only daughter of the relationship by TTY, only to be told that her father had woken her up before he left the house, and told her that her mother was dead and that she had already contacted the Westland police, who were processing the crime scene.

Once the police in Westland knew that Timothy Catalano was at his father's house, they requested that the Sheriff's office in Jackson County, where the father's house was situated, apprehend the fugitive. The arrest was carried out without incident late Monday morning and Catalano was returned to Westland where he was arraigned on Tuesday morning 28 August. He faced charges of homicide-first degree and a firearm felony before Judge Charles Bokos of the 18th District Court.

Timothy Catalano was brought to this police station after his arrest to be charged with the murder of his long-term girlfriend.

Speaking outside the court, Lt. Dan Karrick of the Westland Police Department said that his officers had responded to an emergency call at 1:05 a.m. that morning which came from a house on Gloria Street, Westland. Karrick said that upon arrival, police officers had found a 44-year-old woman named Tammy Lee Susalla unresponsive and suffering from a single gunshot wound to the head. She was still alive, and she was rushed to an area hospital where her condition was stabilised before being flown by helicopter to the University of Michigan Hospital in Ann Arbor, where she died of her wounds early Tuesday morning.

The University of Michigan Hospital in Ann Arbor where Tammy Lee Susalla was taken

During the arraignment, Sergeant Steve Borisch of the Westland Police Department told Judge Bokos that the 20-year-old daughter of the couple, Jessica Catalano, was awakened by her father during the night. He told her that her mother was dead and that he had to leave the house. Upon going to check on her mother, Jessica found her lying on her bed and bleeding severely, and she had immediately called the police on her TTY. Neither Jessica nor her boyfriend, who had been sleeping in the basement of the house, had heard or felt any gunshot. Both were Deaf as well and would not have heard anything.

A search warrant executed on the Gloria Street house recovered two rifles, and Borisch told the court the defendant had indicated to him which rifle had been used in the incident. Through a sign language interpreter, Catalano had told police that Tammy Lee Susalla had been asleep when she was shot in the back of the head.

However, in court, Catalano told Judge Bokos through the interpreter that, "It was an accident, your honour."

A 'not guilty' plea was entered on behalf of Catalano, who was remanded to the Wayne County Jail without bond to return to the court on 6th September for a preliminary hearing, at which it was agreed that Catalano would undergo a psychiatric evaluation.

It took another two years to bring Timothy Catalano to trial. During these two years, he had another referral to the Center for Forensic Psychiatry in Detroit before being found competent to stand trial. His attorney also sought to have his original confession suppressed on the grounds that the confession was made without a competent sign language interpreter.

After Judge Craig Strong rejected the motion to suppress the confession, Catalano entered into a plea agreement with the State Attorney's Office. Under the plea agreement, he pled guilty to the second-degree murder of Tammy Lee Susalla and guilty to felony firearm, which carried a two-year mandatory sentence.

In consequence, Timothy Catalano was sentenced to a minimum of 22 years in prison, with credit for the 749 days he had already served in jail.

Deaf man pleads guilty to killing girlfriend

BY LEANNE ROGERS
OBSERVER STAFF WRITER

In the same week a man was sentenced to life in prison for murdering a Westland woman who had ended their She and Catalano, both deaf, had been a couple for 24 years and shared a home on Gloria, near Merriman and Cherry Hill.

The couple's 19-year-old daughter and her boyfriend unsuccessful defense efforts to have the confession suppressed. The defense also sought to have Catalano found incompetent.

Following two referrals to the Center for Forensic Psychiatry, Catalano was found

Newspaper report of the outcome of the trial

Sergeant Borisch told reporters after the sentencing that he was convinced that the killing of Tammy Lee Susalla was premeditated and worthy of a first-degree murder conviction which would carry a mandatory life sentence without parole. However, he was satisfied with the sentence because when Catalano agreed to a plea agreement, it meant that the family would not have to go through a harrowing court trial, and Catalano would be in his 70s when the time came to release him.

Tammy Lee Susalla's memorial in Parkview Memorial Cemetery
Farmington, Detroit

Chapter 15:

The Abuse
Kaiserslautern, Germany 2007

When Anya Ambos turned to the Internet to find a new partner following the break-up of her marriage to Jens Sänger, which had produced two sons, Lars and Bjorn, she chose a man who was more hard-of-hearing than deaf, wearing a hearing aid to help him get through life. This man, however, had been through a deaf-related education in a mainstream school. As Anya was able to speak very well, and was bilingual in German Sign language as well as spoken German, she was able to relate to him quite well, ignoring the advice of several friends who warned her of his past reputation.

Anya Ambos

Anya Ambos had grown up in a Deaf-environment, boarding in House #5 in the Augustin Violet School for the Deaf in Frankenthal, a town in the Rhineland area of Germany. She had been there from 1975 for two years in the kindergarten class, then from 1977 to 1988 in the main school, during which time she built up a large circle of Deaf friends. There had been a deaf school in Frankenthal since the 19th-century, but the original building was destroyed in a bombing raid in 1943, and the present school was built in its place.

The Augustin Violet School, Frankenthal

Karl Weiss[1], the man Anya met over the Internet, came from Lunen in the North Rhine area of north-west Germany, and the two began to associate as boyfriend-girlfriend, but Anya soon discovered that Karl had a dark side to him. He was very possessive and had a cruel jealous streak, especially when he had been drinking. On several occasions, he imprisoned Anya in his Lunen apartment and refused to let her out. Despite this, Anya continued to associate with him, to the misgivings of her parents Hans and Waltraud Ambos, and her ex-husband, Jens who had custody of the two boys and sometimes withheld access to them from Anya especially if she was in the company of Karl Weiss.

Matters came to a head when Karl and Anya paid a visit to her parents' house in Bruchmühlbach-Miesau, a small town 25 km west of Kaiserslautern on Friday 31 August for a few days stay. As soon as they arrived, Karl started binge-drinking, and later started to verbally abuse Anya's parents and Anya herself. Eventually at 10 am on the morning of Wednesday 5th September, the father, Hans, had enough and bundled him out of the house and into the street, where he continued to drink from a bottle he had taken out of the house with him, and to shout obscenities. Just after lunch and before 2 pm, Karl asked to talk to Anya, who went outside to try and reason with him. Instead, Karl pulled out a knife he had secreted on his body and stabbed Anya.

On hearing his daughter's screams, Hans Ambos ran out of the house to see Karl repeatedly stabbing his daughter, and pushed him off, whereupon Karl ran off as neighbours converged on the stricken woman.

Rheinlandpfalz police recorded the receipt of an emergency call at 1412 hours, and local officers from Bruchmühlbach-Miesau responded immediately to the scene of the stabbing, followed later by detectives from the main headquarters in Kaiserslautern, who put out a BOLO (Be On the Look-Out) for Karl Weiss.

The BOLO described Karl Weiss as 41 years-old, 1.83 metres tall, thin and balding with grey hair, and stubble on his face, dresses in jeans and a denim jacket, wearing a hearing aid in his right ear. The public was warned he might be armed.

Anya Ambos died of her injuries upon arrival at Kaiserslautern's famous Westpfalz-Klinikum GmBH hospital, where they found there were a total of six deep stab wounds inflicted on the upper body. She was 36 years-old at the time of her death.

Barely minutes after the issue of the BOLO, police officers received reports of a man with bloodied clothes and a knife in the streets of Bruchmühlbach-Miesau and managed to apprehend him without a struggle at 1415 hours. He was arrested, informed that his girlfriend was dead, and taken to Kaiserslautern's main police station where he was charged with the murder of Anya Ambos, and retained in custody for psychiatric evaluations.

When the murder of Anya Ambos was announced on German television that evening, the news spread amongst Anya's former schoolmates from Frankenthal like wildfire, and numerous messages expressing shock and condolence for the family were posted on a German deaf web-blog.

A typical message stated: *"I was really shocked by this incident with Anya. I knew her in high school for 12 years. She was my classmate and we were good friends. I last saw her at a reunion in 2002 in Bad Kreuznach."*

Because of the web-blog which gave information where the funeral was to be, Anya Ambos funeral at 2 pm on 11 September was packed with former school friends and classmates.

The newspaper report describing the arrest of Karl Weiss

Karl Weiss appeared in court in Zweibrücken on 22 February 2008 before a jury who found him guilty of the manslaughter of Anya Ambos and sentenced him to eight years imprisonment, a sentence that did not satisfy many of Anya's friends. Weiss had agreed with the state prosecutor Felix Valentin to accept the lesser charge on the proviso that he attended psychiatric sessions for his alcoholic addiction.

Weiss made no acknowledgement of the sentence in court.

The court-house in Zweibrücken where Karl Weiss received a eight-year prison sentence for manslaughter

¹ Karl Weiss is not the man's real name.

It may have been due to the author's poor grasp of German language, but nowhere in any of the newspaper accounts of the case, and of the trial, or in the police press releases, or in the German Deaf web-blog was the name of the murderer stated (although the web-blog clearly showed that a number of bloggers knew the identity of the man).

It was as if it was carefully avoided or deleted. The reason for this is not known.

It was subsequently discovered by the author investigating three other European cases (two of them German) that the press seems to be prohibited from disclosing the names of any victims or murderers. The extract below is a good example of a reported crime that the author was not able to investigate because the names were not known:

> The public prosecutor on Tuesday demanded from the court that the defendant 24-year-old Tayfun Ö be sentenced for ten years for the manslaughter of Fahd T, with eight years and six months juvenile detention for her partner in crime 21-year-old Oguz K. The two deaf defendants had lured Fahd, also deaf, into a sewage tunnel and killed him there with 36 knife wounds.

No surnames, no proper dates, no place names, not even the name of the court, and this was in a German newspaper report! The author came across similar reports in German and Dutch news releases. Such brevity of detail is unhelpful in trying to write about cases!

Similar reports have appeared in Dutch, Turkish and Italian newspapers and it is clear that unless you live in the country itself and know the people concerned, or have access to police sources, you are not going to be able to discover the identities of either the victims or the murderers, or both, and therefore research of the stories would be exceedingly difficult, if not impossible. This is particularly true where an author does not possess fluency of the language in which the newspaper reports or court reports are written.

I was extremely lucky with the story from Poland (Chapter 10) because of the help I got from individuals and library sources within Poland who went to considerable trouble to translate news releases into English. They said they had used it as a translation exercise for students learning English in the library!

I can therefore only apologise to those who would be keen on reading about more stories that happen in Europe for not being able to satisfy their needs.

Chapter 16:

The Seductress
Hong Kong, China 2008

Yip Kai-ming was proud of his standing as a leader in Hong Kong's Deaf Community. Aged 47, he was now a deacon in Hong Kong Deaf People's Christian Church in Kowloon City, helping the Deaf Church's minister, Mr. Ko, to run services regularly and helping to run pastoral services outside the church. These included using his skills as an electrical mechanic to repair electrical appliances in the homes of other churchgoers.

He had been educated in one of Hong Kong's schools for the deaf, the Chun Tok School (usually known as the Hong Kong School for the Deaf). Now aged 47, he was happily married with a Deaf wife and two children.

Through his work with the Deaf Christian Church, Yip met Leung Wai-kong and his wife Ng Kwai-fong in 1989. Yip and Leung had attended the same school, and so had Ng but he had not known her then because of the difference in ages.

Over the years, Yip was a frequent visitor in Leung and Ng's home where the electrical appliances were constantly breaking down, thus necessitating repair. Electrical appliances were expensive in China, and it was the custom to keep them going as long as possible.

Over the years too, Ng made it obvious to Yip that she would like to be intimate with him. Eight years younger than Yip, Ng was still an attractive woman despite having given birth to two children, but Yip was rather pious in his ways. He loved his wife and he loved his work with the church and had no intention of having an affair.

In October 2007, Yip Kai-ming went to Ng's house for yet another repair job, this time a wall-lamp that needed Yip to lift his arms while standing to get to it. Ng greeted Yip at the door wearing only an undergarment, which made Yip uneasy and he asked her to go and get dressed properly. Instead, whilst Yip's back was turned and his arms were raised attending to the repair, Ng came up behind him and embraced him, shoving her hands down the front of his trousers and fondling his genitals.

Having aroused him, Ng set him down on the floor on his back and straddled him, riding him despite his protests that it was a bad thing to do. After the sex act, Yip ran from Ng's apartment as fast as he could. Over the next few months, he avoided Ng as much as he could but one day, he had no choice when Leung asked him to come and repair one of his appliances. When he got there, he found that Leung was not in the house and once again Ng blackmailed him into having sex with her, saying that she would tell his wife he had seduced her. Yip also found that Ng had broken the appliance purposely so that he would be obliged to come to her house.

This happened a third time too, and Yip was in despair. He did not want to lose his wife and his standing in the Deaf community; he also did not want to be with Ng at all and was unhappy about betraying his friend. He told Ng that the sexual liaisons had to stop because he was betraying his wife and his faith.

On September 13 2008, there was once again a broken appliance in the house of Leung Wai-kong and Ng Kwai-fong, and once again, Leung asked him to go and repair it. Suspecting that it was another ruse by Ng to seduce him, he bought a knife and clothes and took them with him to his friend's house, prepared to kill Ng if necessary and destroy the evidence afterwards.

Ng had prepared the way for yet another seduction that day by telling her husband to take the children to her mother's house in Western, a district of Hong Kong where they were to have dinner. She told Leung that she would first go to see an old woman in Tai Po, then go from there to join the rest of the family at her mother's house.

But she did not turn up.

When Leung and the children returned to their home in the Shun Chui Estate in Sha Tin at about 10pm, they found Ng wrapped in a blanket and lying in a pool of blood in the living room and called an ambulance. She had been stabbed several times, and was not breathing. She was pronounced dead at the scene by paramedics.

In the meantime, Yip went into hiding in a park for three days. On the third day, he met the minister of the Deaf church, Mr. Ko, and burst into tears, admitting that he had killed Ng Kwai-fong. He told the minister that Ng had pestered him to divorce his wife and marry her. The minister persuaded Yip to give himself up to the police.

The prosecution rejected Yip's plea of manslaughter and charged him with a full murder indictment. Prior to the trial, Yip's lawyer submitted eight mitigation letters to Judge Michael McMahon, including one from Ng's husband, Leung, who wrote that he had forgiven Yip and believed the blame lay with his wife for seducing Yip. He praised Yip for helping his family in the past.

The Court of the First Instance, Hong Kong

However, the jury in the Court of the First Instance delivered a verdict of guilty but under mitigating circumstances.

Judge Michael McMahon said the jury's verdict showed they believed Yip had acted under duress and that he lost control when Ng touched him. Handing down a sentence of 15 years, McMahon said he had considered Yip's offer to plead guilty to manslaughter – though it was rejected by prosecutors – as well as possible mental and personality problems Yip had and the considerable problems he would face as a deaf person in prison.

Chapter 17:

Gangs of Thieves, Kidnappings and Murders
China 2005-2009

Late in the evening of November 13, 2005, Wang Jinyu, a worker at the Numerical Control School in the Heilongjiang province city of Suihua in the North-east of China, was engrossed in the showing of an excellent television suspense drama when a telephone call brought him back into reality: the telephone call came from a teacher at the Jilin City School for the Deaf and Mute. His daughter Wang Mian, who had started school there only two months previously, had gone missing.

Shocked, Wang Jinyu called his brother Wang Chunmin who had a car and explained the strange call. Together, the two brothers set off that night and drove as quickly as possible to the city of Jilin, which was almost 600 kilometres from Suihua. On the road, Wang Jinyu stared fixedly outside the window, as if the face of his daughter might suddenly appear in the dark and endless night.

Beautiful 14-year-old Wang Mian was born deaf. In order to make sure that their daughter would not "suffer", the parents gathered all their financial resources to see if they could cure her and even gave up their desire to have a second child. As the only daughter with a delicate and pretty face with bright and shiny eyes, the future of Wang Mian had backed her parents into a dilemma -- they could keep her home and guarantee the safety of their daughter, or else give her a good education to equip her for adulthood. After making several inspections of various schools, Wang Jinyu decided to enrol his daughter at the Jilin City School for the Deaf and Mute several hundred miles away, because this was reputed to be just about the best school for the deaf in Northeast China.

"Usually, we don't even want the child to go to the shop in front of the house. We told her again and again not to trust strangers. She is quite obedient. But misfortune still found the child." Wang Jinyu said, really sorry that he had sent his daughter away to study. *"She is so simple and pure, and she cannot speak ..."*

Map of China showing the position of Suihua where the Wangs lived, and Jilin where the school was.
About 500 kilometres separated the two cities.

Wang Jinyu and his brother arrived at the school on the morning of November 14 after driving throughout the night. According to the teacher who had telephoned Wang Jinyu, Wang Mian left school around noon of November 13. She made a sign telling her schoolmates she was going to post a letter. During the study session that evening, she was discovered not to have returned. *"Perhaps she went to an Internet bar, or perhaps she went to a classmate's home."* The teachers said some comforting words. Wang Chunmin noticed that the teachers kept avoiding the use of the words for *"kidnap"* and *"abduction,"* preferring instead to use another phase -- *"getting lost."*

After a fruitless day waiting for news of Wang Mian, a sense of doom enveloped the brothers. Wang Chunmin found the explanations from the school difficult to understand; School principal Lu Hongbo assured them the child would be in no danger. This was a sentence of comfort that actually caused the brothers to become even more disturbed. How could the school really know?

The school claimed to have reported the case to the police, but no police had come to investigate the missing child and it was now over 24 hours since her disappearance

When Wang Chunmin asked the school why the police were not involved, a senior teacher instructed the brothers to go to a conference room, where they found other parents waiting. Other parents? Wang Chunmin then realized that it was more than just Wang Mian who is missing.

It was found that a total of seven students had gone *"missing"* over the last two months --

- On September 4, a 18-year-old female student Yang Zhonghua disappeared after eating lunch;
- On October 16, a 16-year-old male student Guo Qiang disappeared from the school grounds;
- On October 18, a 14-year-old male student Zhang Zhongwu similarly disappeared;
- On November 11, a 16-year-old male student Liu Xiliang and a 15-year-old male student Wang He both disappeared at the same time;
- On November 13, Wang Mian went missing with another 15-year-old female student named Liu Chunyuan.

With seven disappearances, this was simply no longer a case of children *"getting lost."* The first to go missing, Yang Zhonghua, was a member of the work committee at school. A talented drama student, she had participated in national cultural performances of handicapped persons. She came from a single parent home where she did not get enough care and love.

The parents exchanged information about their missing children, and they were all extremely concerned because the four girls were relatively pretty students. The parents found that there had been much abduction of deaf and mute students around the country.

Yang Zhonghua was a talented drama student who had taken part in national dance competitions on behalf of the school

Male students were abducted in order to engage in robbery and theft, but female students were being kidnapped to engage in pornographic activities such as prostitution.

Wang Jinyu was not content with hanging around waiting for news at the school, who were unhelpful. Even the local chief of police, Liu Peizhu, was not interested. Wang Jinyu and the uncle of Liu Chunyuan, 62-year-old Wang Zheng, decided to become conduct their own investigation.

He said later: *"We were trying all sorts of methods to ask around. We heard that there were several deaf and mute girls working as massage girls at a bathhouse in Gongzhuling. So we rushed over. Indeed there were several kids who had been at the Jilin School for the Deaf. There were two males and three females and they were celebrating the birthday of one of the males. They all said that they did not know Wang Mian and Liu Chunyuan."*

When the previously hopeful Wang Zheng heard that, he was deflated. But the birthday boy still gave the two men a little bit of hope when he said that he knew those who were specialising in the abduction of deaf-and-mute students. He promised to send word along to ask for mercy for the missing students. He declined Wang Zheng's offer of 5,000 yuan as payment for his help, and wrote down on a piece of paper, *"All deaf-and-mute people are friends of each other."*

Wang Jinyu and Wang Zheng then hurried to another target location: it was rumoured that there were more than 20 deaf-and-mute persons living in Fanjiachun in Changchun working as thieves. When they got there to the rented house, the neighbours said that the group of people had just left and the people were always very secretive.

On November 16, another parent named Ge arrived at the school. A Deaf coal miner with a Deaf wife, he gestured that his 16-year-old daughter, Ge Chengsong, had disappeared on October 26 and had not been seen since. Because of his deafness and illiteracy, Ge was having communication problems with the police and the school who were both quite unhelpful.

The sudden appearance of Ge caused all the other parents to become even more concerned -- how many more missing Deaf children were there that these parents didn't know about?

At the Jilin School for the Deaf, most of the students were from rural areas, and quite a few came outside the province, such as Wang Mian. Some poor rural families make great economical sacrifices to send their children to the school because of the excellent reputation of the school in the northeast -- in 2005, twenty-seven graduates had entered various universities. The art major at the school was currently ranked one number in the country in terms of graduation rate.

The Jilin School for the Deaf even made outrageous claims that the employment rate for their graduated students was 100%, something that facts did not back up.

Wang Chunmin used to be a communist party secretary in a farm and he was now a businessman, so he could claim to be experienced in the ways of the world. Since he had voiced doubts about what the school was doing many times and he worked with other parents collectively, he sensed that he was not welcomed by the school. Some teachers even advised him to go home. But those honest rural parents came to rely on Wang Chunmin and looked to him to push the school to take action.

After being pressed by the parents, the school finally explained why they remained so calm about the missing school children. According to a senior teacher, more than twenty deaf and mute students had been abducted by criminal deaf-and-mute gangs over the past few years, with things getting especially bad over the past two years. The abduction of deaf-and-mute children happened every year. However, through various connections, the school had been ultimately successful in *"retrieving"* the students. Individual teachers even hinted to some parents to prepare money to *"thank"* people for it. This was because when outside criminal organizations worked with school personnel to abduct the school children, they gave one or two thousand yuan as compensation, which helped to provide the school with necessities it could not otherwise budget for. However, School principal Lu Hongbo denied the existence of the "compensation" phenomenon.

Wang Jinyu and Wang Chunmin were appalled. Was this the Jilin School for the Deaf that they were so satisfied with after inspecting it? They also wondered why such an important issue like abductions needed to be hidden.

Wang Chunmin had quit smoking more than ten years previous, but the stress and the anxiety caused him to start smoking again in Jilin.

By November 15, Wang Chunmin was frustrated with the lack of progress, and then it suddenly occurred to him that he can get the help of the media. So he went to the Jilin reporters' station for the *New Cultural News* and he wanted to get the newspaper to highlight the unsatisfactory state of affairs at the Jilin School for the Deaf.

At 6:45pm, *New Cultural News* reporter Huang Wei had just finished the preliminary interviews and was ready to write his article. He got a piece of good news: the 15-year-old boy, Wang He, who had been missing for four days asked someone to call on his behalf to say that he was abducted and taken to Qingyuanshan district of Liaoning and he had managed to escape from the control of a deaf-and-mute gang.

Huang Wei immediately contacted Wang He's father who rented a car to get to Qingyuanshan which was more than 300 kilometres away from Jilin. The Jilin School for the Deaf and the nearby Zhihuo police station also received the news that Wang He had been found, but neither gave any indication they were pleased. Their attitude caused the various parents to be perplexed, to say the least.

In order to avoid more complications, Wang He's father took a knife and an axe with him in the car.

At some time after 11pm that night, Wang He's father got to where he had been instructed his son was, and saw the sleeping child in a farmer's home in Beiyanggou village. The child seemed to have been beaten in the head and face as there was some swelling. Wang He's aunt went up to embrace him. The sudden movements woke the boy, who thought that danger was upon him and tried to shrivel away. When he saw it was his father and his aunt, he cried with joy.

Through sign language, Wang He said that he and his classmate Liu Xiliang split up in front of the school after class on November 11. He was then kidnapped by four persons who placed clothes over his head. He had more than 100 yuan on him and this was confiscated. He was taken to a place he did not recognise and locked in a room with a barred window, being watched by four persons. Over the next few days, they asked Wang He to steal for them. When he refused, they beat him and did not feed him.

Early morning on November 15, Wang He sneaked out of the house while his captors were asleep. He jumped on a passing lorry and stayed on it as long as possible as he did not know how to get off. When the lorry finally entered a garage, he asked the driver to help him contact his family.

From November 16 onwards, the *New Cultural News* devoted at least one page every day to the case of the missing children. Other provincial media sources also gave publicity. *"What happened to the children?"* became the centre of conversation in the streets of Jilin. On November 17, Jilin province deputy governor and Jilin party secretary Jiao Zhengzhong demanded that the case to be solved with full effort, and the School principal Lu Hongbo was suspended from his post pending the investigation of the case.

According to *New Cultural News*, the police believed that there had to be "insiders" within the school who cooperated with the deaf-and-mute people outside to sell the students. 17-year-old Yang, 19-year-old Chen, 20-year-old Hong and 18-year-old Qu were identified as the important suspects. Qu had been abducted in May earlier that year and had become a key gang member. During interrogation, he told the investigating team that Wang Mian and Liu Chunyuan had been taken away by Huandian City deaf-and-mute persons Wang Lei and Cai Tianxi. During the interrogation, Qu tried to commit suicide by breaking a glass and trying to slice his arm causing the tendon to break. He was trying to use self-mutilation to avoid being questioned.

Yang, Hong and Chen also admitted that they took Wang He and Liu Xiliang to the Jilin train station and handed them over to the deaf-and-mute couple Pu Chengjin and Li Hongliang. At 5pm on November 17, the special squad went to Shulan City Jishu town and arrested Pu Chengin and Li Hongliang. They said that they gave some simple instructions to the kidnapped students and then they re-sold them to other deaf-and-mute burglary rings. They did not know the whereabouts of the children and were arrested.

A police source privately told a friendly local media reporter that their understanding of the situation was that there was more than one abduction group connected to the Jilin school, and that the other missing students might be in the hands of the other criminal organizations. For example, there was deaf-and-mute man named Wang Xuechun who had a criminal record. Wang lived in the Zhihuo district and was suspected of being involved in the cases of the missing children. 42-year-old Wang used to be a student at the Jilin School for the Deaf himself. The police were however unable to find his whereabouts, with Wang having gone into hiding. A teacher who requested anonymity told the newspaper that Wang Xuechun was serving a prison sentence several years back, and while he was in jail, *"the school had a few years of peace"*.

The same evening, school staff were surprised to see a student with a pale complexion wearing a sports jacket and jeans, standing in front of the classroom building. It was Liu Xiliang. He used sign language to inform a teacher: *"They let me wait here."*

Jilin is a north-eastern Chinese city with a severe crime problem; some residents resort to building cages around their cars to prevent theft.

During his questioning, Liu Xiliang never answered the question about "who" they were. The simple message that the boy tried to communicate with all his might was this: he went to Dunhua; he was not beaten; there were a dozen men and women in the house; he was asked to go out and steal but refused. When communication became difficult, Liu Xiliang would shake his head in annoyance, like an impatient lion, and his mouth would emit a low rumble. Even when he first saw his parents again, he expressed only a limited amount of intimacy.

During those two days, the return of the two male students made Wang Jinyu happy, but he was also tormented – his daughter was still missing. On the desk in Wang Mian's bedroom in the school, there were letters from home including her mother's photograph and other personal things. The family back in Suihua called Wang Jinyu in Jilin to say that they had just received the letter that Wang Mian went out to post on the day she disappeared. The Wang family found it hard to bear, and caused Wang Jinyu many sleepless nights in his hotel.

At 2pm on November 18, there were no students to be seen in the corridors of the main building for the School for the Deaf. The iron gates that opened to the classrooms were locked. The parents of the still missing children waited in the conference room. The parents looked at each other. It looked that the waiting of the past few days would continue.

Suddenly, there was pandemonium: *"The missing students are back."* Everybody in the room rushed out.

"Immediately, I saw Chunyuan and another girl (Wang Mian)! They stood so frightened at the door, holding each other up and tears flowing down," said Liu Chunyuan's mother. *"At the time, I could not even stand up straight."* Liu Chunyuan's 18-year-old sister also cried, *"Tomorrow will be grandma's birthday. This is the birthday present that she wants most of all!"*

Wang Jinyu heard the news at his hotel and rushed over. He took Wang Mian into his arms and used his coat and shoulder to cover her up, as if he was afraid that someone might snatch her away again. Seeing so many people around, including press and television reporters with cameras, Wang Mian hid inside the embrace of her father and refused to come out for a long time.

Wang Mian and Liu Chunyuan were quickly sent to the hospital for check-ups, and found not to have suffered any harm. In the subsequent police investigation, the two girls who told how they had been abducted.

According to Liu Chunyuan, their faces were covered outside the school ground and then they were forcibly taken away. Two deaf-and-mute persons took them to Changchun, and then to Harbin. They were locked up in a private home, where several other deaf-and-mute men and women also stayed. The two girls were not asked to do anything. She said that she ran away when the others were not paying attention, and managed get back to Jilin.

In front of their families, Wang Mian and Liu Chunyuan both wrote down their opinions of their abductors: *"Bad people."* Wang Mian said that she was thinking about home and she wanted to go back to school when she was in Harbin.

Compared to the return of Wang He and Liu Xiliang, the sudden appearance of Wang Mian and Liu Chunyuan seemed more mysterious. Why did the Heilongjiang deaf-and-mute group abduct these two girls? Why did they return them? No one had a clear explanation but police believed the publicity created by Wang Chunmin made the gang realise the missing students were too hot to handle and released them.

Later it was found that on the night of November 15, three students under suspicion used an Internet video chatroom (under the supervision of the teachers) to contact a middle person. The three students warned the middle person that the teachers and parents were taking the case of the missing children very seriously. They also lied to say that the police did not know yet, so the children had better be returned quickly.

The fact that Liu Xiliang and others were returned was possibly related to this video chat session. *"Perhaps, this was how the school retrieved the persons previously,"* Wang Chunmin told reporters. He said he had the nagging feeling that the school knew more about the truth of the missing children than people realised.

School principal Lu Hongbo would only admit simply: "In the past, we went through our own connections to find the children. If we did not get them back, given the media hype at this time, wouldn't the parents come to the school? But it usually takes longer to find them, not as quickly as this time."

Wang Chunmin and other parents were perplexed: if the school could coordinate with the criminal organisations to get the students back, why couldn't they ask for police help to eradicate the problem?

The Zhihuo police station refused to discuss the abduction problem at the Jilin School for the Deaf which was within its jurisdiction. A police officer named Lu told reporters that he did not know if the School for the Deaf had ever filed reports and he had no means of contacting the police station director.

During the police investigation, the Jilin School for the Deaf repeatedly told reporters and parents that *"we cannot interfere with the police investigation"* when turning down repeated requests for interviews. The school would not even discuss the educational characteristics of the school or the daily administration of student activities. As the school's supervisor, the Jilin City Department of Education stonewalled inquiries saying that the school's managers were in a meeting out of town.

The school gates remained locked for several days. Visitors were not allowed. Even the vendor who supplied the school cafeteria with bean curds could not deliver the goods. The west side of the School for the Deaf is a brick wall, and the north, east and south sides have iron fences taller than a person. Even during rest days, it was difficult to see students moving in the school. This sealed world was becoming even more isolated and lonely on account of the incident of the missing schoolchildren. Several women who ran businesses in front of the entrance told reporters the school was strict about letting people come in and out, but even so, this did not explain why so many disappearances had happened.

On the afternoon of November 21, just like Wang Mian and Liu Chunyuan, the missing students Guo Qiang and Zhang Zhongwu suddenly appeared at No. 95 Yueshan Road, where the school was located. It was clear that due to the pressure from newspapers about the case, the abductors had released the students.

After a huge fight with the school over withdrawal, Wang Jinyu and Wang Chunmin took Wang Mian home with all her belongings. They admitted that Wang Mian was at the school for only two months, but her writing and sign language expression had progressed amazingly well. But all that was destroyed by four days of nightmare. Other abducted children Wang He, Liu Xiliang, Liu Chunyuan, Guo Qiang and Zhang Zhongwu were also taken back home by their parents. Other children who had not been abducted were also removed by their parents amid fears for their safety. While most of the parents said that they did not want to send the children back to the school, they said that their children must study in a safe environment in order to have a future.

Despite the excellent reputation of Jilin School for the Deaf, it seemed incredible that school had almost become the source for certain criminal organisations.

- Yang Zhonghua and Ge Chengsong were never found. It was rumoured that one or both had been either murdered or sold on to prostitution gangs outside China;
- School principal Lu Hongbo was dismissed from his post by the Jilin City Department of Education, and subsequently arrested by police and sentenced to three years imprisonment for "lack of care and responsibility" to the children in his charge;
- In an effort to try and repair the damage that the missing schoolchildren case caused to the Jilin School for the Deaf, the Prime Minister of China Wen Jiabao made a special visit to the school and held a sign language session with students to show the world what an excellent school the Jilin School was, and to try and give parents confidence in sending their children to the school;
- Intense police activity led to the arrest of many of the leaders of the criminal gangs who had been abducting children not only from the Jilin School, but also from other deaf schools throughout China.

- These children had been press-ganged them into criminal activities. Many of these leaders were themselves Deaf; several were women notably a gang leader named "Big Sister Liu". Many of the gang leaders received prison sentences of up to 13 years;
- Many of the children who were forced into the gangs were released by courts into the custody of their parents without punishment, the courts recognising that the children had acted under duress. Only a few of the abducted children received prison sentences, and this was because these children had taken to the criminal life.

Chinese Prime Minister Wen Jiabao visiting the Jilin School for the Deaf in an attempt to convince parents to return their children to the school.

Despite the publicity and the efforts of the police to arrest the Deaf gang leaders, schools continued to be a source of recruitment through kidnappings and abduction to other Deaf criminal gangs, who used frequent beatings to subdue the children to their will. One such youngster identified only as Yang was abducted from a different school for the deaf and sent to work with a deaf gang in Xining, mid-China. His refusal to take part in gang activities led to him suffering frequent beatings by other gang members, who also refused him food if he did not bow to their wishes.

In the early hours of Sunday 23 August 2009, Yang waited while all the Deaf gang leaders were asleep then taking a machete, he hacked 8 of them as they lay in bed, killing six of them outright and injuring two others. After he had done that, he released all those schoolchildren who were the gang's prisoners and instructed them to go to the police before he fled the house.

When police officers reached the house at 7.20 am that morning, they were met with a scene of carnage. Although the officers recognised many of the dead as criminals they had been hunting for some time, the savagery of the killings forced them to seek out Yang.

When they captured him early Monday morning, Yang wrote that he had suffered much at the gang's hands and so had the other children, and he had done what he did for their sakes.

We do not know what has become of Yang. Given the secrecy in which China conducts its criminal investigations and judiciary practices, this is not surprising. It may well be that as a child himself, he has been spared any death penalty and may have been sent for corrective training.

Chapter 18:

**A rapist poisoned, cut to pieces and burnt
Chimbote, Ancash Province, Peru 2009**

When a group of paramilitary policemen patrolling the Pan-American Highway several kilometres north of the city of Chimbote came upon a group of people acting suspiciously by a car parked by the Kilometre 426 post of the highway, which runs the whole length of the western seaboard of the North, Central and South American continent from Alaska down to Chile, they stopped and asked what they were doing. All of the group immediately pointed to their ears and cried "Sordas!" (deaf in Spanish).

The Pan-American Highway

The fact it was fairly late at night (10 pm) and the spot was isolated and dark, with the group using torches and the lights of their car to communicate made the whole scenario even more suspicious. It was Friday 2 January 2009, and all New Year celebrations should have been over by now. Even more suspicious was a large box in the car which the group of Deaf people were anxious to divert attention from. There was an odd smell coming from the box as well.

None of the policemen understood Peruvian sign language, but by using gestures, one of them gave instructions that the box needed to be opened and inspected.

What they saw inside the box caused some of the policemen to throw up their suppers.

Inside the box, they discovered the cut up parts of a male person. There were the arms, legs, torso and head, most of which were badly burnt.

All the Deaf people present were arrested and transported to the police station in Chimbote; the body parts were also transported to Chimbote where they were delivered to a mortuary for an autopsy.

Chimbote, Ancash Province, Peru

Chimbote is the largest city in Peru's Ancash province, with a population of over 330,000, rising to nearly half-a-million when surrounding villages are counted. Over 80% of the buildings in Chimbote were built after 1970. In that year, South America's most disastrous earthquake struck on 31 May under the sea 20 miles offshore from Chimbote. The earthquake, plus the resulting tsunami, devastated the city and port of Chimbote. Even worse, the earthquake loosened a section of Mount Huascarán, which fell as a massive landslide onto several small towns up the valley from Chimbote and also into a lake that supplied water to the region. Official sources placed the death toll at 74,194 people with another 25,000 missing. Over a million people in the Ancash and neighbouring Huaylas provinces were left homeless. The affected area was larger than Belgium.

Chimbote had a school for the Deaf, which miraculously came through the earthquake and tsunami without being destroyed, although there was some serious damage. The repaired deaf school had a deaf club associated with it that catered for local deaf adults, and after the arrest of the three men and one woman from the car on the Pan-American Highway, they called in personnel from the school and the deaf association who could communicate in sign language to help to interrogate those arrested.

It turned out that all four of them were leading members of the local deaf club, and that two other Deaf women and two other Deaf men who had not been arrested at the scene were also involved in the murder and dismemberment of the body!

Police officers entering the house where the murder and dismemberment took place.

Alexander Chavez, aged 30, Gloria Cesia Walls (40), Ivan Rodriguez (39), Carlos Gonzales (50) – the latter being the car driver – were those arrested with the body parts. Carlos Gonzales was the one who broke ranks, and told the police who the other accomplices were. This resulted in the arrest of Kathy Espino Pereyra (27), Miriam Gerbasi (39) (who was the president of the deaf club), Chuquianqui Gilmer (37) and Torres Duenas (24).

With the help of the communicators from the school and the association, the police uncovered the murder plot. This began when another Deaf member of the deaf club, John Espina Cabello, aged 23, lured Kathy Pereyra into a field on New Year's Eve and brutally raped her.

John Cabello was one of the leading Deaf sportsmen of Peru, winning many trophies which were proudly displayed at the house where he lived with his parents. It would be difficult for Kathy Pereyra to press charges against him, because he was so popular and well known in Chimbote. She told her friends in the deaf club, who agreed that Cabello had to be punished.

The victim, John Espina Cabello

With their connivance, she arranged for Cabello to visit her in her home in the Chimbote suburb of Villa del Mar on the pretence that the rape had to be discussed, holding out also a possibility that a sexual liaison might result that did not need to be part of a rape.

Unknown to Cabello, Kathy Pereyra's house also contained seven conspirators who sought to punish Cabello for the rape. The intention was to drug him with some poisonous gas, but somehow this went wrong and Cabello died from the effects of the poison.

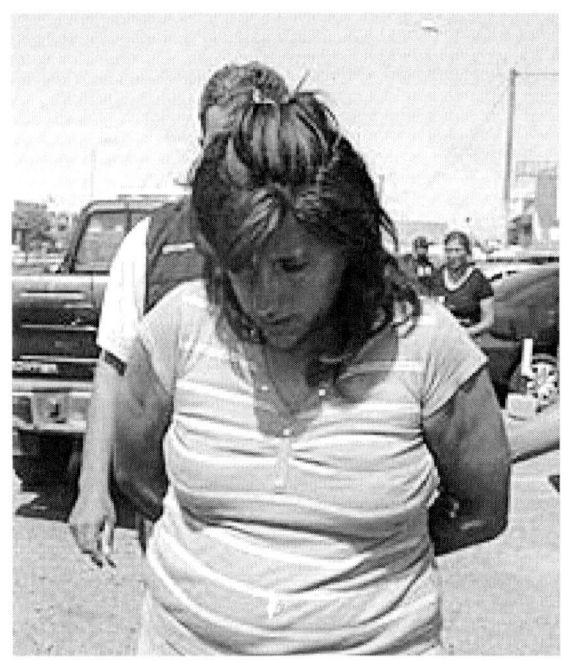

One of the conspirators being led handcuffed into the police station in Chimbote after her arrest

In order to get rid of the body, the conspirators used saws and knives to dismember Cabello, and then tried to burn parts of the body. However, the smell of burning flesh was too much, and they worried about discovery by Kathy Pereyra's neighbours, so they bundled up some of the body parts in blankets and put them inside a box with the intention of disposing of them in the countryside north of Chimbote.

But for the intervention of the paramilitary police patrol, the conspirators might have succeeded in disposing of Johnny Espina Cabello's body, although because of the fact that he was well-known, it might be difficult to conceal his disappearance for long.

At the time of writing (January 2010), none of the Deaf people arrested have yet come to trial. The justice system in Peru is slow, and it is not unusual for people to remain in custody for up to three years. Also, it might be thought the trial would be a nightmare for the justice authorities. There is only one sign language interpreter in Peru who is qualified to work with police or in the courts, and she is based in the capital, Lima, approximately 260 miles south of Chimbote. In order to have a fair trial, each defendant should have access to a different sign language interpreter and lawyer, a logistical issue that could cause huge problems.